# Cambridge Elements

Elements in the History of Constantinople
edited by
Peter Frankopan
*University of Oxford*

# THE GREAT PALACE

Alfredo Calahorra Bartolomé
*Institute of Languages and Cultures
of the Mediterranean and the Near East
(ILC-CCHS-CSIC), Madrid*

Shaftesbury Road, Cambridge CB2 8EA, United Kingdom

One Liberty Plaza, 20th Floor, New York, NY 10006, USA

477 Williamstown Road, Port Melbourne, VIC 3207, Australia

314–321, 3rd Floor, Plot 3, Splendor Forum, Jasola District Centre, New Delhi – 110025, India

103 Penang Road, #05–06/07, Visioncrest Commercial, Singapore 238467

Cambridge University Press is part of Cambridge University Press & Assessment, a department of the University of Cambridge.

We share the University's mission to contribute to society through the pursuit of education, learning and research at the highest international levels of excellence.

www.cambridge.org
Information on this title: www.cambridge.org/9781009675529

DOI: 10.1017/9781009675512

© Alfredo Calahorra Bartolomé 2026

This publication is in copyright. Subject to statutory exception and to the provisions of relevant collective licensing agreements, no reproduction of any part may take place without the written permission of Cambridge University Press & Assessment.

When citing this work, please include a reference to the DOI 10.1017/9781009675512

First published 2026

*A catalogue record for this publication is available from the British Library*

ISBN 978-1-009-67552-9 Hardback
ISBN 978-1-009-67548-2 Paperback
ISSN 2514-3891 (online)
ISSN 2514-3883 (print)

Additional resources for this publication at www.cambridge.org/calahorra

Cambridge University Press & Assessment has no responsibility for the persistence or accuracy of URLs for external or third-party internet websites referred to in this publication and does not guarantee that any content on such websites is, or will remain, accurate or appropriate.

For EU product safety concerns, contact us at Calle de José Abascal, 56, 1°, 28003 Madrid, Spain, or email eugpsr@cambridge.org

# The Great Palace

Elements in the History of Constantinople

DOI: 10.1017/9781009675512
First published online: January 2026

Alfredo Calahorra Bartolomé
*Institute of Languages and Cultures of the Mediterranean and the Near East (ILC-CCHS-CSIC), Madrid*

Author for correspondence: Alfredo Calahorra Bartolomé,
alfredo.calahorra@cchs.csic.es

**Abstract:** The Great Palace of Constantinople was the heart of Byzantium for almost a thousand years, serving as both a political and architectural model for Christendom and the Islamic world. Despite its historical significance, reconstructing its layout remains challenging due to the scarce amount of archaeological evidence. This Element synthesises the historical and topographical evolution of the palace, examining its architectural typologies and the role of ritual and artistic objects in representing imperial power. It also addresses key historiographical issues, such as the identification and dating of the Peristyle of the Mosaics, as well as its role in imperial ceremonies. The research is based on textual sources, archaeology, and graphic documentation, culminating in a virtual reconstruction through 3D imaging. By integrating these methodologies, this Element aims to offer a comprehensive understanding of the Great Palace, its influence, and its role as a central stage for Byzantine ceremonial and ideological expression.

**Keywords:** Great Palace, Constantinople, ceremonies, architecture, 3D reconstruction

© Alfredo Calahorra Bartolomé 2026

ISBNs: 9781009675529 (HB), 9781009675482 (PB), 9781009675512 (OC)
ISSNs: 2514-3891 (online), 2514-3883 (print)

## Contents

1  Introduction and Methodology                    1

2  Evidence for the Study of the Palace            4

3  The Upper Palace                                7

4  The Lower Palace                               59

Bibliography                                      88

An online supplementary material is available at
www.cambridge.org/calahorra

## 1 Introduction and Methodology

The Great Palace of Constantinople served as the residence of the Byzantine emperors for a millennium and stands as one of the most significant examples of aulic architecture during the Late Roman and medieval periods. The objective of this Element is to provide a comprehensive examination of the palatial complex, addressing specific challenges along the way.[1]

The Great Palace was located at the southeastern corner of the Byzantine peninsula, within the first region of Constantinople, in close proximity to the city's most prominent monumental landmarks, such as Hagia Sophia, the Hippodrome, the Augoustaion square, and the Baths of Zeuxippos. From the first hill, the complex descended southward down the slope, towards the shore of the Marmara Sea. This was achieved by a series of artificial terraces. The total area of the complex encompassed approximately 16 hectares. However, the palace would only reach such dimensions through successive expansions. The original core, known as Daphne, was established by Constantine (r. 306–337) at the same time as the construction of his new capital. Situated in the upper part of the hill, it was adjacent to the Hippodrome. Upon entering the palace through the Chalke – its main gate, located near the Great Church – one would encounter the barracks of the guard, arranged across several porticoes. Beyond the barracks were various significant halls dating back to the Late Antique period, including the Augousteus, the Nineteen Couches, and the Consistory. This palace remained the heart of the imperial residence until the sixth century, when it gradually ceded importance to the lower complex, by the seashore. The Lower Palace was the result of the amalgamation of several noble residences, such as the Palace of Hormisdas and the houses of various Theodosian princesses. By the tenth century, the Chrysotriklinos had become the focal point of this complex, around which were situated the imperial private quarters, the palatine churches of the Pharos Terrace, and the maritime façade known as Boukoleon.

Prior to embarking upon the study of the palace, it is important to mention some of the main approaches to the complex. In the mid nineteenth century, Jules Labarte is credited with the first comprehensive modern study of the palace.[2] At the turn of the century, subsequent authors, such as Jean Ebersolt, integrated a more meticulous analysis of the sources with first-hand knowledge of the area's topography.[3] In

---

[1] This Element is an abridged and simplified version of an extensive doctoral thesis written between 2018 and 2023, titled 'Keleusate: arquitectura, arte y ceremonia en el Gran Palacio de Constantinopla'. The full thesis is expected to be published in due course, with an English translation planned for the future.

[2] Jules Labarte, *Le Palais impérial de Constantinople et ses abords, Sainte Sophie, le Forum Augustéon et l'Hippodrome, tels qu'ils existaient au Xe siècle* (Paris: Victor Didron, 1861).

[3] Jean Ebersolt, *Le Grand Palais de Constantinople et le Livre des Cérémonies* (Paris: Ernest Leroux, 1910).

the mid twentieth century, significant archaeological findings were made, which will be discussed in Section 3.9.1. Rodolphe Guilland's studies from this period were particularly noteworthy, despite being limited to textual analysis.[4] Cyril Mango's book on the Chalke Gate, published around that time, represents one of the most significant approaches to the palace, integrating, for the first time, analysis of archaeological, textual, and visual sources.[5] In the subsequent decades, there was a shift towards prioritising the analysis of archaeological remains over a broader study of the palace. From the 1990s onwards, along with the beginning of new excavations, there has been a revival of interest in the palace from a topographical and typological perspective. In this context, some of the most noteworthy authors include Jan Kostenec, Jonathan Bardill, Michael Featherstone, Albrecht Berger, and Nigel Westbrook, with the latter offering the most recent interpretation of the palace.[6]

The primary objective of the present approach is to elucidate the historical development and functional evolution of the palace buildings, with the ultimate goal of establishing a topographically coherent layout of the ensemble (Plan 2 – hypothetical). For this purpose, it will be necessary to examine a range of sources, including archaeological, written, and visual materials. Once the location and features of the structures have been identified, they will be compared with better-known examples in order to determine their appearance and possible typological parallels. Some of the preceding approaches to the palace have been complemented by reconstructive drawings and, in more recent times, by 3D virtual reconstructions, such as the one found in the Byzantium1200 project.[7] For this approach a new reconstruction has likewise been created (Figure 1), with the goal of conveying a general idea of the palace

---

[4] Rodolphe Guilland, *Études de topographie de Constantinople byzantine*, 2 vols. (Berlin: Adolf Hakkert, 1969).

[5] Cyril Mango, *The Brazen House: A Study on the Vestibule of the Imperial Palace of Constantinople* (Copenhagen: I kommission hos Munksgaard, 1959).

[6] J an Kostenec, 'The Heart of the Empire: The Great Palace of the Byzantine Emperors Reconsidered', in Ken Dark (ed.), *Secular Buildings and the Archaeology of Everyday Life in the Byzantine Empire* (Oxbow: Oxbow Books, 2004), 4–36; Jonathan Bardill, 'Visualizing the Great Palace of the Byzantine Emperors at Constantinople: Archaeology, Text, and Topography', in Franz A. Bauer (ed.), *Visualisierungen von Herrschaft: Frühmittelalterliche Residenzen – Gestalt und Zeremoniell; Internationales Kolloquium 3./4. Juni 2004 in Istanbul* (Istanbul: Ege Yayınları, 2006), 5–46; Michael Featherstone, 'The Great Palace as Reflected in De Cerimoniis', in *Visualisierungen von Herrschaft*, 47–61; Michael Featherstone, 'The Everyday Palace in the Tenth Century', in Michael Featherstone *et al.* (eds.), *The Emperor's House: Palaces from Augustus to the Age of Absolutism* (Berlin: De Gruyter, 2015), 149–158; Albrecht Berger, 'The Byzantine Court as Physical Space', in Ayla Ödekan *et al.* (eds.), *The Byzantine Court: Source of Power and Culture: Papers from the Second International Sevgi Gönül Byzantine Studies Symposium* (Istanbul: Koç University Press, 2010), 12–22; Nigel Westbrook, *The Great Palace of Constantinople: An Architectural Interpretation* (Turnhout: Brepols, 2019).

[7] www.byzantium1200.com/, retrieved 3 January 2021.

**Figure 1** 3D reconstruction of the Great Palace of Constantinople in the tenth century. Author.

and its layout, including decorative elements and furnishings, which are essential for the understanding of medieval architecture.

## 2 Evidence for the Study of the Palace

### 2.1 Archaeological Evidence

A comparison of the entire area occupied by the palace with the surviving evidence may lead to the conclusion that the archaeological remains are scarce (Plan 1 – archaeological). On occasion, Ottoman buildings, such as the Blue Mosque, have been erected over areas previously occupied by some central elements of the complex, such as the Constantinian Daphne. Nonetheless, some significant ensembles have survived, like the façade of the Boukoleon over the Marmara, while others of great relevance have been excavated, such as the mosaic peristyle or the Chalke Gate. Consequently, the archaeological remains should be regarded as the primary source of information for a topographical study of the palace. The first comprehensive archaeological survey of the area is credited to Ernest Mamboury and Theodor Wiegand, who documented much of the Byzantine evidence that emerged in the eastern end of the peninsula at the beginning of the twentieth century. Of particular interest are the remains found beneath the Palace of Justice, which burned down in 1933. The surveyed areas labelled as Mamboury Aa, Ab, and Ac comprised the infrastructure of what were once the Palace Gate, barracks, administrative offices, and a series of galleries that traversed the palace from north to south. Further south, the team proceeded along the galleries towards the Marmara Sea and documented the Mamboury B, featuring a polygonal apse and the sole standing structure of the Upper Palace, a *kochlias* or spiral staircase known as the Ramp House. Continuing southward, the Mamboury D group, which comprised additional galleries, the infrastructure of a rectangular chamber, and a cistern, hinted at the next significant discovery in the area: the mosaic peristyle.[8]

The peristyle was discovered in 1935 by a British team. The war interrupted the excavations, which were resumed in 1952 and confirmed that a large apsed hall overlooked the eastern side of the courtyard.[9] In the 1980s and 1990s, a team from the Austrian Academy of Sciences undertook the appropriate restoration of the peristyle and transformed it into a museum.[10] The

---

[8] Ernest Mamboury and Theodor Wiegand, *Die Kaiserpaläste von Konstantinopel zwischen Hippodrom und Marmara-Meer* (Berlin: De Gruyter, 1934).

[9] Gerard Brett *et al.*, *The Great Palace of the Byzantine Emperors: Being a First Report on the Excavations Carried Out in Istanbul on Behalf of the Walker Trust (The University of St. Andrews) 1935–1938* (Oxford: Oxford University Press, 1947); David Talbot Rice, *The Great Palace of the Byzantine Emperors: Second Report* (Edinburgh: Edinburgh University Press, 1958).

[10] Werner Jobst *et al.*, *Istanbul: The Great Palace Mosaic* (Istanbul: Arkeoloji ve Sanat Yayınları, 1997).

archaeological site was notable not only for its size, comparable in plan to that of Hagia Sophia, but also for the mosaic that adorned the four porticoes forming the peristyle. Despite the significance of the discovery, there is currently no consensus regarding the dating, patronage, and identity of the complex.

Over the past few decades, Turkish archaeologists have been particularly active in the area surrounding the Palace of Justice. The excavation of the Mamboury Aa complex was resumed, with the uncovering of the Chalke Gate and a chapel. In a northward direction, parallel to Hagia Sophia, significant findings were made, including the apse of another chapel, Late Roman mosaics, a bath complex dating to the reign of Justinian (r. 527–565), and infrastructures featuring frescoes, likely associated with the Magnaura.[11] It is similarly important to acknowledge the contributions of Eugenia Bolognesi, who initiated a comprehensive review, regrettably unfinished, of all the archaeological remains of the palace. However, she provided one of the most crucial insights for studying the ensemble: the systematisation of the terraces upon which the palace was raised.[12]

## 2.2 Written Sources

The most extensive body of information about the palace is derived from written sources. Among them, the most significant is the *Book of Ceremonies*, which was compiled in the mid tenth century at the behest of Constantine VII (r. 913–959). The emperor, raised as a hostage in the palace, was aware of the crucial role that ceremonies played in reflecting the integrity of the imperial institution. This was defined by the Byzantines as order, *taxis*, a key concept of imperial discourse. Therefore, the purpose of the *Book of Ceremonies* is to compile the imperial ritual to ensure its accurate execution and transmission to future generations, thus maintaining the harmony of the State.[13]

---

[11] Çiğdem Girgin, 'La porte monumentale trouvée dans les fouilles près de l'ancienne prison de Sultanahmet', *Anatolia Antiqua* 16 (2008): 259–290.

[12] Eugenia Bolognesi, 'Il Gran Palazzo', *Bizantinistica* 2 (2000): 197–242; between 1993 and 2007, she published a series of articles in *Araştırma Sonuçları Toplantıları* regarding various archaeological sites related to the palace.

[13] The most recent edition, with a French translation, is *Constantin VII Porphyrogénète: Le Livre des Cérémonies, Corpus Fontium Historiae Byzantinae* 52, 6 vols., edited and translated by Gilbert Dagron and Bernard Flusin (Paris: Association des amis du Centre d'Histoire et Civilisation de Byzance, 2020); for convenience, I have used the English translation in *Constantine Porphyrogennetos: The Book of Ceremonies*, 2 vols., translated by Ann Moffat and Maxeme Tall (Canberra: Australian Association for Byzantine Studies, 2012). For imperial ceremonies, see Christian Rollinger, *Zeremoniell und Herrschaft in der Spätantike: Die Rituale des Kaiserhofs in Konstantinopel* (Stuttgart: Franz Steiner Verlag, 2024); Michael McCormick, 'Analyzing Imperial Ceremonies', *Jahrbuch der Österreichischen Byzantinistik* 35 (1985): 1–20; Sabine G. MacCormack, *Art and Ceremony in Late Antiquity* (Berkeley: University of California Press, 1981).

The *Book of Ceremonies* is the result of a revision undertaken during the reign of Nicephorus II Phocas (r. 963–969). It consists of two books. The first one begins with religious ceremonies, describing the major fixed feasts, such as Christmas. It then proceeds to the movable ones, and some of particular interest to the Macedonian dynasty, such as the inauguration of the Nea Ekklesia. Subsequently, the text proceeds to delineate civil ceremonies: coronations, wedding rites, and promotions. Finally, we find the protocols necessary for the Hippodrome and the emperor's interaction with the factions. The first book ends with a fragment from a lost work by Peter the Patrician, a contemporary of Justinian. The second book begins with some chapters that follow the organisation of the first volume, featuring processions, receptions, and promotions. However, the structure becomes increasingly complex thereafter, likely due to the inclusion of materials that were never properly organised, such as rituals illustrated with historical events, a brief history of the Byzantine emperors, a list of imperial tombs, inventories of palace warehouses, and salary lists. Finally, a manual for banquets composed in 899, the *Kletorologion* of Philotheos, and a list of bishoprics, attributed to Epiphanius of Salamis, were appended.

The importance of the *Book of Ceremonies* for the understanding of the palace lies in the method chosen to systematise the rituals, which was based on a detailed account of processions. This required a meticulous description of the itineraries through the palace, detailing in strict order the connections between the halls, chambers, and galleries. The *Book of Ceremonies* also addresses logistics and ornamentation, describing the veils, thrones, tables, and couches displayed during banquets and audiences, as well as the lamps and precious objects that were hung from arches and domes. This is important not only in its own right but also because it often provides additional insights into the architecture, such as the number of arches or the presence of an apse. Thus, after a proper interpretation of the itineraries, we can achieve a reasonably accurate depiction of the palace as it stood at the time of the compilation.

However, the *Book of Ceremonies* has its limitations: it was written by and for individuals familiar with the palace, and it never mentions anything that is not absolutely necessary. Therefore, we have to rely on other sources, such as histories, topographic records, and travel accounts. Some important texts in this regard, including detailed descriptions of the palace, are *Theophanes Continuatus*, the *Patria of Constantinople*, and the *Embassy* of Liudprand, bishop of Cremona, among many others.

## 2.3 Visual Evidence

Although little remains of the palace, visual representations of certain buildings have survived. Some of these, such as the Late Antique base of the Egyptian obelisk or the twelfth-century Madrid Scylitzes manuscript (BNE, VITR/26/2), are contemporaneous with the complex and are therefore of considerable importance. However, most of them date from the Ottoman period, when Turkish miniaturists and Western travellers shared a common interest in recording the ruined monuments of the Byzantine past, which they regarded as both marvellous and exotic. Notable examples include the maps by Cristoforo Buondelmonti and Matrakçi Nasuh, engravings by Pieter Coecke Van Aelst and Willey Reveley, and even daguerreotypes, such as Pierre Tremaux's 1850 photograph of the Boukoleon balcony.

## 3 The Upper Palace

According to Bolognesi, the Upper Palace was built on three terraces:

(a) At 32 and 31 m.a.s.l. stood the main avenue of the city, the Mese, the Hippodrome, the Baths of Zeuxippos, and the Augoustaion square. In addition, the Chalke Gate and the Palace of Daphne were situated at the same level, along with the barracks of the guard and the administrative offices. This area roughly corresponds to Atmeydanı Square, Sultan Ahmet Park, the Four Seasons Hotel and its surroundings, and the Blue Mosque.
(b) At 26 m.a.s.l., on the eastern flank of the palace, the Mamboury galleries B and D, as well as the peristyle of the mosaics, can be found. These structures run through Kutlugun Sk. and Akbiyik Cd., where remnants of some of them, like the Ramp House, are still visible. The museum of the mosaics is situated beneath the southeastern corner of the Blue Mosque, within the present-day Arasta Bazaar.
(c) At 21 m.a.s.l., Bolognesi documented the floor of the infrastructure that supported the previous buildings. This level would have served as a transition between the Upper and Lower Palaces.[14]

Besides the presence of these levels, it is essential to highlight that the Upper Palace was organised along two axes, one to the west and another to the east. This allows for a systematic study of the upper complex. Starting from the

---

[14] Eugenia Bolognesi, 'The Great Palace of Constantinople: An Introduction to the Main Areas of Activity, Ground Levels and Phases of Development', in Werner Jobst *et al.* (eds.), *Neue Forschungen und Restaurierungen im Byzantinischen Kaiserpalast von Istanbul: Akten der Internationalen Fachtagung vom 6.-8. November 1991* (Vienna: Österreichische Akademie der Wissenschaften, 1999), 9–10.

original core, we will follow these routes clockwise until we return to our starting point. The western route will take us through Daphne and the Kathisma, the Tribunal and the Nineteen Couches, the barracks of the *scholarioi* and the *exkoubitores*, and the Chalke Gate. Upon reaching the northernmost point in the Magnaura, we will descend along the eastern axis, passing through the Ovaton, the barracks of the *kandidatoi*, and the peristyle of the mosaics. Subsequently, we will return to the vicinity of Daphne, at the courtyard known as the Covered Hippodrome. Finally, we will address the expansions of the Upper Palace over the centuries (Figure 2).

## 3.1 Daphne

Although not explicitly stated in the sources, it is thought that Daphne was the original core established by Constantine, and it is already documented in the fifth century. Its name likely originates from the triumphant symbolism associated with laurel wreaths in Late Antiquity. This is corroborated by the denomination of some of the buildings that were part of the complex, such as the chapel of St Stephen (his name coinciding with the word for crown or wreath), the portico of the Gold Hand, and the *Stepsimon* or coronation hall. The complex became emblematic, subsequently serving as a model for the imperial palace in Ravenna, which was given the same name (*ad Laureta*) (Figure 3).[15] Nothing remains of Daphne and its neighbouring structures, and the Blue Mosque now stands on its former site.

Initially, the term Daphne may have encompassed the entire palace. However, by the tenth century, it referred only to the Augousteus *triklinos* (audience or banqueting hall) and adjacent rooms. At that time, the complex continued to serve as a significant ceremonial venue, although the emperor's main residence had already shifted to the Lower Palace. Access to the Augousteus was gained from the Covered Hippodrome or the Triconch via a series of internal galleries.[16] Before reaching the hall, adjacent to the Galleries of Daphne, two chapels were located, one consecrated to the Virgin and another to the Trinity. It is known that both chapels were connected to each other, and that the latter had an adjoining chamber where relics were kept. Further on was the baptistery.[17] The Augousteus was the main audience hall of the foundational complex. It was closely associated with the emperor's residence, and he would frequently traverse it to reach his private chamber in Daphne, to access the Kathisma of the Hippodrome, or, alternatively, to reach the grand portico of the Upper Palace, known as the

---

[15] Alfredo Calahorra, 'On the Toponymics of the Great Palace of Constantinople: The Daphne', *Byzantinische Zeitschrift* 115 (2022): 1–29.
[16] *Book of Ceremonies*, 573, 584.   [17] *Ibid.*, 7–8, 71, 72, 129, 162–163, 174, 176, 180, 304.

**Figure 2** View of the Upper Palace. Author.

**Figure 3** Mosaic of the *Palatium* in Sant'Apollinare Nuovo, Ravenna, sixth century. Wikimedia Commons.

**Figure 4** View of the Tribunal, with the Augousteus and its portico, the Gold Hand, and the *triklinos* of the Nineteen Couches. Author.

Tribunal (Figure 4). The Augousteus plays a pivotal role in the *Book of Ceremonies*, serving as the venue for the coronation of the empress and the solemn appearance of the emperor, already crowned, before the court. Consequently, it is referred to as *Stepsimon*, *Stepahana*, or Domus Coronaria.[18]

---

[18] *Accounts of Medieval Constantinople: The Patria*, translated by Albrecht Berger (Washington, DC: Dumbarton Oaks Research Library and Collection, 2013), 1, 59; *The Complete Works of Liudprand of Cremona*, translated by Paolo Squatriti (Washington, DC: Catholic University of America Press, 2007), *The Embassy of Liudprand*, 3.

We know some details about the Augousteus's structure and elements. The assembly of courtiers was typically arranged in a Π-shaped configuration, which suggests a rectangular plan.[19] It is beyond doubt that an apse was present at the southern end of the structure.[20] The aforementioned internal galleries must have reached the *triklinos* from its eastern side, as the chapels had to be oriented in this direction. It is also known with certainty that the Octagon, situated adjacent to the Augousteus in the west, served as a dressing room where the *cubicularii* (attendants of the imperial bedchamber) attired the emperor prior to his appearance before the court.[21] To the north, the hall opened onto the portico of the Gold Hand in the Tribunal through a single great door, from which curtains bearing designs of birds were hung.[22] Thanks to these clarifications, it can be inferred that the Augousteus had a rectangular plan with an apse and opened onto a portico. In summary, it had the canonical appearance of a typical triclinium from Late Antiquity, exactly like the one unearthed by the mosaic peristyle.[23] Furthermore, the presence of additional structures suggests that the building had a north–south orientation.

As previously stated, the western side of the Augousteus provided access to the Octagon. Besides its function as a dressing room, the Octagon also served to distribute access to several spaces. The emperor's private chamber was situated on one side of the building, while the chapel of St Stephen was located on the opposite side.[24] Looking west, this chapel, or more likely a passageway connected to it, led to the spiral staircase leading to the Kathisma of the Hippodrome.[25] St Stephen was the most important chapel in Daphne. Originally, it was used as a winter chamber but was later consecrated to the First Martyr by Pulcheria (r. 450–453).[26] Its primary function was to host the imperial wedding liturgy and the blessing of water on Epiphany. Inside the chapel were preserved the Cross of Constantine, sceptres, diptychs, and gold insignias belonging to the *kandidatoi*.[27] The only known feature of the structure is a narthex.[28]

---

[19] *Book of Ceremonies*, 69, 136.  [20] *Ibid.*, 208.
[21] *Ibid.*, 7–9, 21, 26, 33, 69, 136, 141, 143, 146–147, 176, 197, 203, 208, 212, 214, 362, 583, 593.
[22] *Ibid.*, 9, 69, 72, 129, 136, 205, 209–210, 214, 232.
[23] On this typology, see Jean-Pierre Sodini, 'Habitat de l'antiquité tardive (1)', *Topoi* 5, 1 (1995): 151–218; Jean-Pierre Sodini, 'Habitat de l'antiquité tardive (2)', *Topoi* 7, 2 (1997): 435–577; Luke Lavan, 'Late Antique Governors' Palaces: A Gazetteer', *Antiquité Tardive* 7 (2000): 135–164; and Ken Dark, 'Roman Architecture in the Great Palace of the Byzantine Emperors at Constantinople during the Sixth to Ninth Centuries', *Byzantion* 77 (2007): 87–105
[24] *Book of Ceremonies*, 9, 21, 26 1st schol., 71–72, 129, 136, 140, 143, 163, 176, 204.
[25] *Ibid.*, 208, 304, 309, 342, 347, 362.
[26] *Patria*, 1, 59; *The Chronicle of Theophanes Confessor: Byzantine and Near Eastern History, AD 284–813*, translated with introduction and commentary by Cyril Mango and Roger Scott (Oxford: Clarendon Press, 1997), AM 5920.
[27] *Book of Ceremonies*, 8–9, 640.  [28] *Ibid.*, 178.

## 3.2 The Kathisma

In Rome, the Palatine Hill overlooked the valley of the Circus Maximus. The propaganda potential of connecting the circus to the Palace was quickly recognised by the emperors. Augustus (r. 27 BC–AD 14) erected the original Pulvinar, which Trajan (r. 98–117) later transformed into a monumental tribune. By the late third century and during the Tetrarchic period, the hippodrome–palace formula had already been established, with significant examples such as the urban palaces of the Sessorium in Rome, Milan, Sirmium, Thessalonica, Nicomedia, and Antioch, as well as the villa of Maxentius along the Appian Way.[29] While historical accounts agree in suggesting Constantine's desire to emulate Rome, his construction of a palace adjacent to the circus merely reflected the customs of his era. In Constantinople, the imperial box overlooking the circus was designated as Kathisma and remained in use, albeit deteriorated, until the late twelfth century.[30] It is probable that it was destroyed by fire in 1204.[31]

The Kathisma was situated on the eastern flank of the Hippodrome, although its precise location remains a matter of debate. The majority of authors posit that the Kathisma stood in front of one of the main monuments of the arena, such as the Egyptian obelisk, the bronze serpent, or the masonry obelisk. The latter appears to be the most plausible hypothesis, as the masonry colossus stands in front of a thick pillar of the Hippodrome's infrastructure (Mamboury H1), and because it is the sole monument of the *spina* (a central strip dividing the arena of a circus) mentioned in connection with the Kathisma (Figure 5).[32]

Arriving from the Galleries of St Stephen, one would reach the *kochlias*. The original staircase, being too narrow for imperial processions, was enlarged by Justinian.[33] Upon ascending, the emperor would not arrive at the intermediate level but rather at the uppermost one, designated as the *parakyptika* (overlooking galleries). From this point, he could observe the arena privately, behind a screen. Once the preparations had been completed, he descended via a stone staircase to a private chamber on the main level. There, the *cubicularii* dressed him in the chlamys and crown. Afterwards, he passed through a small dining

---

[29] John H. Humphrey, *Roman Circuses: Arenas for Chariot Racing* (London: Batsford, 1986).

[30] *O City of Byzantium: Annals of Niketas Choniates*, translated by Harry J. Magoulias (Detroit: Wayne State University Press, 1984), Andron1, 1, 290.

[31] Concerning the Hippodrome, see another title within the Cambridge Elements in the History of Constantinople series: Engin Akyürek, *The Hippodrome of Constantinople* (Cambridge: Cambridge University Press, 2021).

[32] Mamboury and Wiegand, *Kaiserpaläste*, 43–44; *Book of Ceremonies*, 366; Jean-Claude Golvin and Fabricia Fauquet, 'L'hippodrome de Constantinople: Essais de restitution architecturale du dernier état du monument', *Antiquité Tardive* 15 (2007): 207–208.

[33] *Procopius, with an English Translation*, 6 vols., translated by Henry B. Dewing (London: William Heinemann, 1914–1940), *Persian War*, 1, 24, 43; *Book of Ceremonies*, 391.

**Figure 5** View of the Kathisma. Author.

room to reach the great dining hall, where he was greeted by the court. Finally, the large door leading to the imperial box would open and the emperor sat on his throne to watch the races. The box and the flanking porticoes of the senators were also reformed under Justinian, shortly after his accession to the throne, in 528.[34] Upon returning to the palace, the emperor could access the *kochlias* directly without having to ascend to the *parakyptika*.[35]

The lower level of the Kathisma on the circus side was known as *skamma*, *stama*, or Π. This name referred to the recessed area in front of the imperial box, where athletes contended and victorious charioteers received their prizes. Sometimes this area is also referred to as Daphne of the Hippodrome, after the laurel wreaths awarded to the victors.[36] The Karea Gate, which opened onto the Hippodrome, led through a passage to the Covered Hippodrome, within the palace. The denomination of this gate likely originated from a nearby statue of Artemis, as it coincided with the name of the main festival of the goddess in the Peloponnese.[37]

Due to its public nature and its connection with the Hippodrome, the Kathisma is among the most visually documented monuments of the palace. Consequently, we can picture the exterior appearance of the Kathisma and

---

[34] *The Chronicle of Marcellinus*, with a translation and commentary by Brian Croke (Sydney: Australian Association for Byzantine Studies, 1995), AD 528.
[35] *Ibid.*, 304–309, 316, 324–325, 342–344, 361–364, 758, 774, 778, 781.
[36] Calahorra, 'The Daphne', 29–45.
[37] Liudprand, *Embassy*, 2; Niketas Choniates, *Annals*, Andron1, 2, 346; *Nicholas Mesarites: His Life and Works in Translation*, translated with notes and commentary by Michael Angold (Liverpool: Liverpool University Press, 2017), *Coup of John the Fat*, 8; *Patria*, 2, 74.

**Figure 6** Kathisma of the Hippodrome in a fresco from St Sophia in Kiev, eleventh century. Wikimedia Commons.

visualise many of its elements as described in the sources. In addition to the well-known bases of Theodosius's obelisk, evidence from the 5th and 6th centuries includes the bases of the monuments celebrating the charioteer Porphyrius, the Kugelspiel of Berlin, and various consular diptychs featuring the *stama*. Their medieval counterparts are the eleventh-century fresco from Hagia Sophia in Kiev (Figure 6) and the miniatures from the Scylitzes manuscript (fols. 55 r–55 v). The different levels of the Kathisma are depicted in these artefacts with the main floor featuring the imperial throne, its canopy, and, in the background, an arcade under which the courtiers stand. On the upper level we can clearly observe the *parakyptika* with the lattice. These images also represent some of the changes undergone by the Kathisma. For instance, in the earliest examples, we can see multiple gates and staircases ascending from the arena to the upper levels. Except for the Karea, these features are absent in the Kiev fresco, having been suppressed by Justinian after the Nika riots.[38]

### 3.3 The Tribunal and the Gold Hand

The Tribunal was the main porticoed courtyard (*exaeron*, *araia*) of the Upper Palace (Figure 4).[39] It was overlooked by the Augousteus and the *triklinos* of the

---

[38] *Patria*, 3, 201.  [39] *Book of Ceremonies*, 20, 211–212, 218–219, 222, 226.

Nineteen Couches, the former from the portico of the Gold Hand, to the south, and the latter from the portico of the Nineteen Couches, to the west.[40] The *triklinoi* of the guard, namely, the hall of the *kandidatoi* to the east and the halls of the *exkoubitores* and the *scholarioi* to the north, protected the Tribunal from the remaining sides. The main function of the Tribunal was to provide an open space for the courtiers and the palatine regiments to assemble and acclaim the emperors. In this regard, we know that the dances of the circus factions were celebrated there until the reign of Heraclius (r. 610–641).[41]

The most significant feature of the Tribunal was the Gold Hand, that is, the southern portico of the courtyard. Its columns were made of polychrome marbles taken as *spolia* from Delphi. At its centre stood the *dikionion*, a monumental porch with two columns that led to the Augousteus. While the origin of its name remains unknown, the Gold Hand is undoubtedly related to the coronation rituals and the Daphne complex. When the crowned emperors left the adjoining hall through the great door, they stood beneath the *dikionion*, flanked by patricians and senators. The veil hanging from the columns was then removed, and the emperor was acclaimed by the court gathered in the Tribunal.[42]

### 3.4 The *Triklinos* of the Nineteen Couches

The largest hall in the palace was the *triklinos* of the Nineteen Couches (Figure 4). Since its foundation, its primary function was to host banquets held by the emperor. The hall was constructed by Constantine, and it may have been operational as early as 325, as the celebrations accompanying the Council of Nicaea were held there. At that time, it was already characterised by the succession of couches placed on each side and the splendid coffered ceiling adorned with jewelled crosses.[43] It served a number of other purposes, including the display of the deceased emperors.[44] The southern end of the *triklinos*, where the imperial table was placed, was aligned with the portico of the Gold Hand, to which it was connected through a door. This section of the hall stood above several steps and was separated from the rest of the space by a railing adorned with silver columns.[45] The most significant pieces of evidence about the location of the

---

[40] *The History of Theophylact Simocatta*, translated by Mary Whitby and Michael Whitby (Oxford: Clarendon Press, 1986), 1, 1, 1 and 1, 10, 2.

[41] *Patria*, 2, 32.

[42] Calahorra, 'The Daphne', 3, 11–29. Berger and Kostenec have argued that the Augousteus did not open onto the Tribunal and that its portico was the Onopodion, a different courtyard within the palace, Kostenec, 'Heart of the Empire', 4–13. This interpretation contradicts texts from the *Book of Ceremonies* like 26, 2nd schol., 161 or descriptions like that of Simocates quoted earlier in this section.

[43] *Eusebius: Life of Constantine*, introduction, translation, and commentary by Averil Cameron and Stuart G. Hall (Oxford: Clarendon Press, 1999), 3, 10, 11 and 15, 1–2.

[44] *Book of Ceremonies*, 275–276.   [45] *Ibid.*, 25.

**Figure 7** A banquet featuring *akoubita* and sigma-shaped tables from the *Book of Job*, eleventh century. Monastery of St Catherine, Sinai, Cod. Sin. Gr. 3, fol. 17v. From Weitzmann, Kurt and Galavaris, George, *The Monastery of Saint Catherine at Mount Sinai: The Illuminated Greek Manuscripts*. Vol. 1 (Princeton: Princeton University Press, 1990), pl. 17, fig. b.

banquet hall are that, as previously stated, it overlooked the Tribunal and that, according to Liudprand, it was very close to, or even adjoining, the Hippodrome, with a north–south orientation.[46] The Nineteen Couches remained in use until the tenth century, when it was restored by Constantine VII, who added a new coffered ceiling composed of octagons carved with gilded vine leaves.[47] From this point onwards, the hall is no longer mentioned in the sources.

As inferred from its name, this *triklinos* was renowned for its distinctive arrangement of nineteen tables with a sigma shape, where guests would dine while reclining on couches (*akoubita*), following the ancient Roman custom (Figure 7). The emperor's table was situated at one end, while the remaining eighteen tables were arranged on either side, in two rows of nine tables facing each other. With twelve guests per table, the total number amounted 228. Courtiers were arranged hierarchically, both on their couches and the hall, with proximity to the emperor indicating the person's importance.[48] Foreign dignitaries frequently attended these gatherings, which featured various spectacles: Liudprand of Cremona and Harun ibn-Yahya described the tableware, all of gold and silver, and how the food was transported along the hall in large golden vessels, so heavy that they had to be carried on carts guided by a pulley

---

[46] *The Complete Works of Liudprand of Cremona, Retribution*, 6, 8.
[47] *The Rise and Fall of Nikephoros II Phokas*, notes and translation by Denis Sullivan (Leiden: Brill, 2018), *Theophanes Continuatus* Book 6, Years 944–961, 450.
[48] *Book of Ceremonies*, 726–741; Simon Malmberg, 'Visualising Hierarchy at Imperial Banquets', in Wendy Mayer and Silke Trzcionka (eds.), *Feast, Fast or Famine. Food and Drink in Byzantium* (Leiden: Brill, 2005), 11–24.

mechanism hanging from the ceiling. Singers entertained during the dinner, while the evening concluded with a series of balancing acts and acrobatics.[49]

The typology of this hall has been the subject of significant debate regarding terminological and morphological issues. The problem was first raised by Richard Krautheimer, who proposed that, around the year 800, Pope Leo III (r. 795–816) copied the Nineteen Couches in his eleven-apsed triclinium in the Lateran Palace. After comparing the ritual and the furniture, he concluded that the Nineteen Couches must have also had nineteen apses. To this day, authors such as Martin Luchterhandt, Kostenec, or Westbrook have supported this theory.[50] Others, like Simon Malmberg, Isabella Baldini-Lippolis, and Salvatore Cosentino, lean towards a strictly basilical solution, without lateral apses.[51]

Regarding terminology, it is important to point out that the mention of *akoubita* and sigma-shaped tables does not imply the existence of apses, as can be seen in some *trapezai* (refectories) on Mount Athos, which follow the model established in the Great Lavra by St Athanasios in the tenth century. Moreover, not a single text mentions the presence of apses in the hall. In fact, Liudprand states that the name of the Nineteen Couches 'did not emerge from the structure itself'.[52] In any case, the papal protocols cited by Krautheimer do not refer to the eleven-apsed basilica but rather another hall known as the Basilica Magna, which only had three apses. Consequently, the comparison is purely superficial.

To complete our morphological characterisation of the Nineteen Couches, it is also important to consider how it was connected to the Tribunal. As it was the largest hall in the palace, scholars have often placed it in a central position, presiding over the Tribunal, and have even associated it with the *dikionion*, thus displacing the Augousteus. However, the Nineteen Couches did not have

---

[49] Liudprand, *Retribution*, 6, 8–9; Alexander Vasiliev, 'Harun ibn-Yahya and his description of Constantinople', *Seminarium Kondakovianum* 5 (1932): 157–158; *Book of Ceremonies*, 754–757.

[50] Richard Krautheimer, 'Die Dekaenncakkubita in Konstantinopel: Ein kleiner Beitrag zur Frage Rom und Byzanz', in Richard Krautheimer, *Ausgewählte Aufsätze zur europäischen Kunstgeschichte* (Cologne: Dumont, 1988), 195–199; Martin Luchterhandt, 'Päpstlicher Palastbau und höfisches Zeremoniell unter Leo III.', in Christoph Stiegemann and Matthias Wemhoff (eds.), *799. Kunst und Kultur der Karolingerzeit. Karl der Große und Leo III.* (Mainz: Philipp von Zabern, 1999), 109–122; Kostenec, 'Heart of the Empire', 4–9; Westbrook, *Great Palace*, 111–120.

[51] Simon Malmberg, 'Dazzling Dining: Banquets as an Expression of Imperial Legitimacy', in Kalirroe Linardou and Leslie Brubaker (eds.), *Eat, Drink and Be Merry (Luke 12:19): Food and Wine in Byzantium. Papers of the 37th Annual Spring Symposium of Byzantine Studies, in Honour of Professor A.A.M. Bryer* (Aldershot: Ashgate, 2007), 75–91; Isabella Baldini-Lippolis and Salvatore Cosentino, 'Rituali di corte: Il Triclinio dei XIX Letti del Grande Palazzo di Costantinopoli', *Byzantinische Zeitschrift* 114, 1 (2021): 65–110.

[52] Liudprand, *Retribution*, 6, 8.

**Figure 8** The Basilica of Constantine in Trier, early fourth century. Wikimedia Commons.

a frontal access but rather a lateral one. The *triklinos* had only two entrances, one to the north and the other to the south, next to the imperial couch.[53] Given that the hall was adjacent to the circus and oriented in a north–south direction, the only feasible solution would be to place the doors on the eastern side. This configuration resembles strictly contemporary examples consisting of large basilicas laterally attached to porticoes, as in the Tetrarchic palaces of Sirmium, Milan, and, especially, Thessaloniki. The latter is an exact parallel to the present interpretation of the Nineteen Couches.[54] It also has nine recesses on each side, likely implying the presence of windows and, maybe, couches. This is a feature shared by the Constantinian basilica in Trier as well (Figure 8). This conclusion is of significant importance, as it not only assists in visualising the Nineteen Couches but could also contribute to a more accurate characterisation of the functions of these grand structures, which are often described as audience halls. Given their size and morphology, it is more likely that they were banquet halls, just like the Nineteen Couches in Constantinople (Figure 9).

---

[53] *Book of Ceremonies*, 209, 214, 381ff. Next to the southern door was the office of the *kastresios*, the official in charge of organising banquets, *ibid.*, 211.

[54] Fani Athanasiou *et al.*, 'Η Βασιλική του Γαλεριανού Συγκροτήματος', *Αρχαιολογικό Έργο στη Μακεδονία και Θράκη* 12 (1998): 113–126.

**Figure 9** The *triklinos* of the Nineteen Couches. Author.

## 3.5 The Barracks of the Imperial Guard

As in most royal residences, in Constantinople barracks stretched between the private and ceremonial quarters and the main gate. The barracks consisted of a succession of porticoes, cubicles, and monuments, which not only served as living quarters for the soldiers but also housed various administrative offices. This area is broadly referred to as the Scholai, from the Latin *schola*, meaning a small room, in reference to the aforementioned *cubicula*.[55] The barracks were built by Constantine but burned down during the Nika Revolt and were later rebuilt by Justinian.[56]

It has been mentioned that the *triklinoi* of the three corps of palatine troops were adjacent to the Tribunal. The hall of the *kandidatoi* was attached to the

---

[55] Eugenia Bolognesi, 'The Scholae of the Master of the Offices as the Palace Praetorium', *Anatolia Antiqua* 16 (2008): 231–257.
[56] *Patria*, 1, 59; *Procopius, with an English Translation, On Buildings*, 1, 10.

eastern portico of the court, serving as a connection with the eastern itinerary, while those of the *exkoubitores* and the *scholarioi* were adjacent to the northern portico. The first monument on the way to the gate, also adjacent to the northern side of the Tribunal, was the Dome of the Lamps or Heptakandelon. Its name derived from the ceremonial display featuring a *menorah* upon which the Mandylion of Edessa was hung.[57] This superimposition might have represented the fulfilment of the Old Testament promises through the incarnation of Christ.

One exited the Lamps through the Great Gate of the Exkoubitores, which led to the Curtains.[58] It is unclear whether this refers to an actual veil hanging above the gate or a portico adorned with drapes. Nearby stood a stable, as the emperor enjoyed the privilege to ride up to this place after crossing the Chalke.[59] After passing through the Curtains, one would reach the first Schola, presided over by the Rotunda of the Eight Columns. This building must have been ancient, as it was also known as the Old Mint.[60] Its form and alleged early date of construction suggest that it was likely a Constantinian structure, and thus might have resembled various Late Antique centralised typologies, such as the mausoleum of Diocletian and the treasury of the palace in Sirmium.[61]

Although we know there should have been seven Scholai, one for each regiment, apart from the first, only the fifth is mentioned in the *Book of Ceremonies*.[62] Nearby stood the last significant monument before reaching the Palace Gate, the Church of the Holy Apostles, which may also have been the work of Constantine. Its dedication coincides with that of his mausoleum, and we know that the emperor took great care to ensure his bodyguards were Christians.[63]

### 3.6 The Chalke Gate and Its Surroundings

Constantine constructed a vestibule for his palace, which he surmounted with a painting depicting the emperor and his sons slaying a serpent symbolising Licinius.[64] A visual representation of this propylaeum may be achieved by comparing it with the vestibule of Theodoric's palace in Ravenna, as depicted in

---

[57] *Book of Ceremonies*, 8 1st schol., 12–13, 20, 27, 35, 40, 252, 265; *Patria*, 1, 59.
[58] *Book of Ceremonies*, 84, 99, 107, 168, 270, 810.   [59] *Ibid.*, 32, 84, 99, 107, 572.
[60] *Ibid.*, 8, 11, 131, 572, 579.
[61] Mark J. Johnson, *Roman Imperial Mausoleum in Late Antiquity* (Cambridge: Cambridge University Press, 2014), 59–70; Ivana Popović, 'Porphyry sculptures from Sirmium', *Antiquité Tardive* 24 (2016): 373–374.
[62] *Book of Ceremonies*, 131.
[63] *Ibid.*, 19, 36, 40, 252; Eusebius, *Life of Constantine*, 1, 8 and 4, 17–21.   [64] *Ibid.*, 3, 3.

Sant'Apollinare Nuovo (Figure 3). This construction might have emulated the one in Constantinople and was also known as Chalke. However, the Constantinian gate was destroyed during a revolt in Anastasius's reign (r. 491–518), around 495. He assumed the reconstruction of the edifice, but it was subsequently destroyed during the Nika riots of 532.[65] The ruins that we know today correspond to the final reconstruction undertaken by Justinian. Although it predates this period, it is from that moment onwards when its designation, Chalke, became popular. The term was used to describe either the grand bronze doors or the roof, made from the same material. In the Byzantine period, the gate led directly to the Mese, the main avenue of the city. This initial section of the street was known as the Regia and featured two-storey porticoes (Figure 10). At the far end stood the Milion, a triumphal arch in the shape of a *tetrapylon* (*quadrifrons* triumphal arch). This layout followed a typical scheme found in Late Antique urban palaces, as evidenced in Split or Antioch.[66]

The ruins of the main gate of the palace lay under the remains of the Ottoman Palace of Justice, between the eastern boundary of Sultanahmet Square and the Four Seasons Hotel. After the fire that destroyed it, in 1933, Mamboury surveyed the area and labelled it as zone Aa.[67] Between 1997 and 2008, a Turkish team conducted extensive excavations east of Sultanahmet Square and Hagia Sophia. Successive campaigns uncovered the remains of the Gate, which Mango had placed in the same location fifty years earlier.[68]

The excavations revealed a rectangular courtyard. The western enclosing wall, 2.5 m thick, was pierced by a large gate over 6 m wide. On either side of the gate, two thick pillars projecting from the wall indicated the presence of the vestibule. Flanking these pillars, the courtyard wall was adorned with niches and columns standing on marble steps. On the northern wall of the courtyard, a smaller vestibule was uncovered, opening onto a narrow passage. It had a rectangular plan and a two-arched entrance supported by a marble pillar. A small rectangular chapel was attached to the south wall.[69]

The discovered ruins accurately match Procopius's description: the Gate had the plan of an almost square rectangle. From each of the corners, a thick pillar ascended. The two eastern pillars projected from the enclosing wall, as it has been revealed in the course of excavations. Above, four arches spanned between each of the four pillars. The resulting space between the pillars and these arches

---

[65] Mark J. Johnson, 'Towards a History of Theoderic's Building Programme', *Dumbarton Oaks Papers* 42 (1988): 73–96.
[66] Slobodan Ćurčić, 'Late-Antique Palaces: The Meaning of Urban Context', *Ars Orientalis* 33 (1993): 67–90.
[67] Mamboury and Wiegand, *Kaiserpaläste*, 35–36.   [68] Mango, *Brazen House*, figure 1.
[69] Girgin, 'La porte monumentale', 259–290.

**Figure 10** The Chalke Gate and its surroundings, including the Magnaura and the Church of the Saviour. Wikimedia Commons.

**Figure 11** Interior of the Chalke Gate. Author.

was closed with four pendentives, upon which rose a dome. The decoration comprised polychrome marbles and mosaics, depicting the victories of Belisarius, contemplated by Justinian and Theodora, who, surrounded by the court, stood at the centre of the dome (Figure 11).[70] This architectural model corresponds to a typology widespread in the Late Antique Mediterranean, known as projecting porch. It was likely present in the vestibule erected in Cartagena by Comentiolus, Byzantine governor of Spain, and is well documented in the Islamic sphere with examples from the palaces of Amman and Khirbat al-Mafjar, in the Levant, and Ajdabiya, in Libya.

The remaining elements unearthed are also mentioned in the sources. The porticoed gallery flanking the vestibule was known as the *peripatos*. The northern, smaller porch was known as the Iron Gate, while the chapel to the south was likely the one erected by Romanus Lecapenus (r. 920–944) in honour of Christ

---

[70] Procopius, *On Buildings*, 1, 10.

**Figure 12** The Church of the Saviour in the 1790s, engraving by Gugas Inciciyan, from Eyice, 'Arslanhane ve Çevresinin Arkeolojisi', figure 4.

the Saviour. In close proximity to this chapel, John Tzimisces (r. 969–976) constructed another, larger one, with the same dedication.[71] It featured two semi-domes and a large central dome, and was probably standing on a platform that gave the church additional height. Several representations of the structure exist, including Nasuh's map of Istanbul, Reveley's view of Hagia Sophia, and an engraving by Gugas Inciciyan (Figure 12). The building was demolished in 1804, and no remains have been discovered.[72]

Being the main public façade of the palace, the Chalke became a showcase of imperial will. For instance, upon the declaration of war, weapons and shields were hung from the gate.[73] In this regard, the Chalke played a crucial role in demonstrating the emperors' support for either the iconoclastic or orthodox faction. According to tradition, an icon of Christ had presided over the Chalke Gate since at least the reign of Maurice (r. 582–602). Leo III (r. 717–741) is said to have dismantled it to express his rejection of icons. Nowadays, it is widely acknowledged that this account is likely apocryphal. It is believed that Irene (r. 769–802) installed the mosaic of Christ above the gate for the first time. The icon was then dismantled by Leo V (r. 813–820), only to be definitively restored by Theodora (r. 830–856) in 843, marking the Triumph of Orthodoxy.[74] While its dating and attribution are controversial, the Trier ivory, depicting

---

[71] *Book of Ceremonies*, 19, 27, 35, 39; *Patria*, 2, 28 and 3, 213.
[72] Mango, *Brazen House*, 149–169; Neslihan Asutay-Effenberger and Arne Effenberger, 'Zur Kirche auf einem Kupferstich von Gugas İnciciyan und zum Standort der Chalke-Kirche', *Byzantinische Zeitschrift* 97, 1 (2008): 51–94.
[73] *Book of Ceremonies*, 458.
[74] Marie-France Auzépy, 'La destruction de l'icône du Christ par Léon III: Propagande ou réalité?', *Byzantion* 60 (1990): 445–492; Brubaker and John Haldon, *Byzantium in the Iconoclast Era, c. 680–850: A History* (Cambridge: Cambridge University Press, 2011), 128–135; Brubaker, *Inventing Byzantine Iconoclasm* (London: Bristol Classical Press, 2012), 27–31.

**Figure 13** The Trier Ivory, mid ninth century. Treasury of the Cathedral. Wikimedia Commons.

a translation of relics, likely portrays the Chalke Gate and the two-storied portico of the Regia around that time (Figure 13).[75]

Following the iconoclastic period, the Chalke Gate assumed additional roles, functioning as a court of justice and a prison.[76] Emperor Isaac II (r. 1185–1195) removed the bronze doors, but the vestibule survived the Byzantine Empire, albeit in a ruined state.[77] This is how we see it in various representations, such as the *Nuremberg Chronicle* and an engraving by Van Aelst.[78] The building may have been finally demolished in the first half of the seventeenth century, likely to salvage materials.[79]

### 3.7 The Great *Triklinos* of the Magnaura

During the Middle Byzantine period, the Magnaura served as the primary audience hall of the palace. It also accommodated part of the imperial wedding ceremony, the emperors' public addresses during Lent, a court of justice, and a government-sponsored school.[80] Despite its importance, it was situated

---

[75] Alfredo Calahorra, 'El marfil de Tréveris una iconografía clave en el contexto de la propaganda político-religiosa del Triunfo de la Ortodoxia', *Erytheia* 39 (2018): 9–53, a revised and improved English version will be published in 2025.

[76] Mango, *Brazen House*, 21–35.    [77] Niketas Choniates, *Annals,* Isaac2, 3, 442–443.

[78] Jonathan Berger and Albrecht Bardill, 'The Representations of Constantinople in Hartmann Schedel's World Chronicle, and Related Pictures', *Byzantine and Modern Greek Studies* 22 (1998): 1–37.

[79] Tülay Artan, 'The Making of the Sublime Porte Near the Alay Köskü and a Tour of a Grand Vizierial Palace at Sülemaniye', *Turcica* 43 (2011): 162.

[80] Palatine ceremonies are described in the *Book of Ceremonies*. For the court of justice, see *John Scylitzes. A Synopsis of Byzantine History, 811–1057*, translated with introduction, text, and notes by John Wortley (Cambridge: Cambridge University Press, 2010), Bas1, 16; for the school,

outside the palace, adjoining the complex at its northern end. It was close to Hagia Sophia, approximately parallel to the Augoustaion square, which gave its name to one of the gates leading out of the Magnaura complex.[81] The hall itself stood on a semicircular terrace constructed in the early seventh century, together with a commemorative column and an armoury.[82] The monumental complex was completed during the reign of Heraclius.[83] The curvature of this terrace can still be discerned along the İshak Paşa Cd. ramp as it ascends towards Hagia Sophia. Some archaeological remains may be associated with the relative position of the Magnaura. Of particular note is a basement dating back to the sixth century, which was later embellished with frescoes in the 8th and 9th centuries.[84] Also noteworthy is the presence of a cistern that, according to written sources, might have been the same that provided delicious fish for the emperor's table.[85]

The *Patria* state that the hall's name originated from the cry uttered by the elderly Emperor Anastasius upon his death, as he was caught in a thunderstorm: 'O mother (*mana*), I perish by the breeze (*aura*) [of fire]'.[86] However, it is merely an adaptation of the Latin *Magna Aula*. Although the construction of the Magnaura is traditionally attributed to Constantine, it achieved its greatest

---

The Chronicle of the Logothete, translated with introduction, commentary, and indices by Staffan Wahlgren (Liverpool: Liverpool University Press, 2019), 130, 35; *Joseph Genesius. On the Reigns of the Emperors*, translation and commentary by Anthony Kaldellis (Canberra: Australian Association for Byzantine Studies, 1998), 4, 17; *Chronographiae quae Theophanis Continuati nomine fertur Libri I–IV, Corpus Fontium Historiae Byzantinae* 53, edited and translated by Michael Featherstone and Juan Signes Codoñer (Berlin: De Gruyter 2015), 4, 26–29. For its significance in the history of Byzantine learning, Paul Lemerle, *Le premier humanisme byzantin: Notes et remarques sur enseignement et culture à Byzance, des origines au Xe siècle* (Paris: Presses Universitaires de France, 1971), 148–176.

[81] *Book of Ceremonies*, 214.

[82] Sources like Theophanes, *Chronicle*, AM 6088, Symeon, *Chronicle*, 108, 6 and *Patria*, 2, 34 disagree as to whether the constructor of the terrace was Maurice or Phocas.

[83] *The Greek Anthology, with an English Translation*, 5 vols., translated by William R. Patton (London: W. Heinemann, 1916–1918), 9, 655.

[84] Alpay Pasinli, 'La zona settentrionale del Gran Palazzo: Interventi di scavo. Il Giardino della vecchia prigione di Sultanahmet', in Eugenia Bolognesi (ed.), *Il Gran Palazzo degli Imperatori di Bisanzio* (Rome: Istituto Italiano di Cultura di Istanbul, 2000), 37–42; Asuman Denker et al., 'Former Sultanahmet Prison', in Selmin Kangal (ed.), *Istanbul: 8000 Years Brought to Daylight. Marmaray, Metro, Sultanahmet Excavations* (Istanbul: Koç University Press, 2007), 139–141; Asuman Denker, 'Excavations at the Great Palace', in *The Byzantine Court*, 13–15; Asuman Denker, 'Great Palace (Büyuk Saray)', in Asuman Denker (ed.), *Byzantine Palaces in Istanbul* (Istanbul: Istanbul Arkeoloji Müzeleri, 2011), 23.

[85] Alpay Pasinli, 'Pittakia ve Magnum Palatium-Büyük Saray Bölgesinde 1999 Yili Çalışmaları (Eski Sultanahmet Cezaevi Bahçesi)', *Müze Çalışmaları* 11 (2001): 44; *Chronographiae quae Theophanis Continuati nomine fertur Liber quo Vita Basilii Imperatoris amplectitur, Corpus Fontium Historiae Byzantinae* 42, edited and translated by Ihor Ševčenko (Berlin: De Gruyter, 2011), 92.

[86] *Patria*, 3, 180.

renown during the 9th and 10th centuries, when it hosted memorable state receptions for foreign ambassadors.[87]

The location and date of the complex have stirred controversy regarding its possible identification with the Senate of the Augoustaion, reconstructed by Justinian following the Nika riots, as proposed by Mango (Figure 10).[88] Other scholars, such as Rudolf Stichel, posit that the Curia and the Magnaura were distinct buildings.[89] The argument put forth by this author is based on the presence of monumental columns in the Augoustaion, which are purported to match those described by Procopius as adorning the Senate's porch. Nevertheless, it is known that a considerable number of commemorative columns stood in the Augoustaion.[90] Furthermore, the Senate did not directly open onto it; instead, it was situated on the other side of the street or square running east of the Augoustaion, the Pittakia, whose main feature was the column of Eudoxia.[91] The base of this monument was discovered to the southeast of Hagia Sophia and can be seen today in the garden of the Great Church. Aside from its location, the most compelling evidence supporting the identification of Senate and Magnaura arises from the correspondence between the morphology described in independent historical sources and the *Book of Ceremonies*.

Describing the hall's morphology is a complex task. While traditional views support a three-aisled basilica, Berger, for instance, has proposed the possibility of a central dome.[92] According to the sources, the complex consisted of two elements: the *triklinos* itself and a porticoed courtyard planted with trees known as *anadendradion*. The Magnaura had a conch at the eastern end, beneath which the emperor's throne was placed. The presence of a conch is also highlighted in the accounts describing the Senate of the Augoustaion.[93] The throne was the most characteristic element of the hall and was designed to emulate the throne of King Solomon, from which it took its name. It was situated behind a railing, above a flight of steps, and flanked by automata shaped like lions. These figures

---

[87] *Ibid.*, 1, 60.   [88] Mango, *Brazen House*, 57–58.

[89] Rudolf Stichel, 'Sechs kolossale Säulen nahe der Hagia Sophia und die Curia Justinians am Augusteion in Konstantinopel', *Architectura* 30 (2000): 1–25.

[90] Mango, *Brazen House*, 42–47; the columns mentioned by Stichel purportedly bore signs of the Zodiac, a fact corroborated in the Augoustaion, *Patria*, 1, 49.

[91] *Socrate de Constantinople: Histoire ecclésiastique*, 4 vols., introduction, notes, and translation by Paul Maraval and Pierre Périchon (Paris: Éditions du Cerf, 2004–2007), 6, 18; *Sozomène. Histoire ecclésiastique*, 4 vols., introduction, notes, and translation by André-Jean Festugière, Bernard Grillet, and Guy Sabbah (Paris: Éditions du Cerf, 1983), 8, 20; *Patria*, 2, 31.

[92] Albrecht Berger, 'Die Senate von Konstantinopel', *Boreas* 18 (1995): 131–142.

[93] *Book of Ceremonies*, 199–200, 213, 215, 545, 567; *The Chronicle of John Malalas*, a translation by Elizabeth Jeffreys *et al.* (Canberra: Australian Association for Byzantine Studies, 1986), 13, 8; *Chronicon Paschale 284–628*, translated with introduction and notes by Mary Whitby and Michael Whitby (Liverpool: Liverpool University Press, 1989), AD 328.

could stand, roar, and move their tails. A tree of gold with singing birds stood above the ensemble, and a mechanism allowed the enthroned emperor to ascend to the ceiling of the hall. The entire spectacle would unfold as the thunderous organs filled the air.[94] Regarding the hall itself, we only know that it had a rectangular floor plan, as evidenced by the fact that two rows of seven lamps were hung there during receptions, indicating two short sides to the east and west, and two long sides to the north and south.[95] A bedchamber was adjacent to the building.[96]

The façade of the Magnaura was notable for its porch, which, according to the *Book of Ceremonies*, consisted of four large columns and a great arch.[97] This is consistent with Procopius's description of the Senate's porch, which comprised two pilasters adjacent to the wall and four immense columns of white marble supporting a vault.[98] Under this arch, a green marble *omphalion* (circular marble plaque) marked the emperor's position during ceremonies.[99] From there, a monumental flight of stairs led to the garden. Courtiers, bodyguards, and leaders of the circus factions would be arranged on these steps in hierarchical order, flanking the emperor, who stood on the highest step. The courtyard had two porticoes, and a row of trees, the actual *anadendradion* (garden), which was decorated with chains, silks, precious objects, and lamps, as if they were colonnades. The northern portico was adjacent to the empress's stable, while the southern one led to the palace through a bridge. The western end of the courtyard opened to the public thoroughfare by the aforementioned Gate of the Augoustaion.[100] This side was closed off by the *anabasion*, a raised passage built by Justinian, which allowed access from the palace to the Great Church. The *anabasion* started at the Iron Gate of the Chalke, in a place called Chytos, and led to the southeastern gallery of Hagia Sophia, through a door that now opens to the void.[101] A portion of this passage can be observed in the engraving of the *Nuremberg Chronicle* and in Matrakçı Nasuh's map of Istanbul.[102]

During excavations in the vicinity of the Chalke Gate, a polygonal apse was uncovered in an area corresponding to the space between the Magnaura and the Augoustaion. This structure plausibly aligns with the Chapel of the Varangians, also known as the Chapel of the Patricians. According to Byzantine sources, it

---

[94] *Book of Ceremonies*, 566–569; Liudprand, *Retribution*, 6, 5; Allegra Iafrate, *The Wandering Throne of Solomon* (Leiden: Brill, 2016), 55–105.
[95] *Book of Ceremonies*, 570.   [96] *Ibid.*, 138, 567.   [97] *Ibid.*, 570–571.
[98] Procopius, *On Buildings*, 1, 10, 6.   [99] *Book of Ceremonies*, 155.
[100] *Ibid.*, 155, 197, 200–201, 213–216, 260, 547, 567, 571, 583–584, 593.
[101] Mango, *Brazen House*, 85–92.
[102] Berger and Bardill, 'The Representations of Constantinople', 16–17, 20.

## The Great Palace

was located behind Hagia Sophia, between the Chalke Gate and the Chapel of the Holy Well, exactly where the apse was found.[103]

### 3.8 The Eastern Itinerary: The Galleries of Eros and the Triklinos of the Ovaton

As mentioned in the introduction, the entire eastern flank of the palace is lined with the remains of galleries running north–south:

(a) The first ensemble of relevance consists of a thick wall made of stone ashlar, which must have formed the southern end of the Magnaura's terrace. This wall bordered a street 40 m long and 4 m wide. The Mamboury Ac2 group was situated directly south of the street, already within the palace proper. It comprised a terrace formed by a network of chambers separated by brick cruciform pillars. Further south, the Mamboury Ab group marks the actual beginning of the galleries heading southward.[104]

(b) These galleries extended to the Mamboury B complex, whose main feature is the Ramp House (Ba), a *kochlias* or three-storey spiral staircase divided into nine sections, which gave access to one of the upper terraces of the palace, at 26 m.a.s.l (Figure 14). A small apse on the upper level suggests the presence of a chapel. A few metres northwest of the ramp, the foundations of a grand polygonal apse (Bc) were documented, surrounded by galleries (Bb) and cisterns (Bd). Further south, a series of passages led to a fountain (Bg). Near this source, the remains of a ramp similar to Ba were also documented, but practically destroyed (Be). From here, after creating a recess, the galleries proceeded southward until reaching the next significant complex, Mamboury D.[105]

The itinerary corresponding to these remains is designated by the *Book of Ceremonies* as the passageways leading to the Hall of Eros, one of the southernmost chambers of the Upper Palace.[106] This route is fairly well documented, especially thanks to the bridal ritual, which allows for many identifications. Firstly, it must be noted that a street separated the area ascribed to the Magnaura

---

[103] Pasinli, 'Pittakia ve Magnum Palatium-Büyük Saray Bölgesinde 2000 Yili Çalışmaları (Eski Sultanahmet Cezaevi Bahçesi)', *Müze Çalışmaları* 12 (2002): 5; Raymond Janin, *La géographie ecclésiastique de l'Empire Byzantin, Le siège de Constantinople et le patriarcat oecuménique, vol. 3: Les églises et les monastères* (Paris: Institut Français d'Études Byzantines, 1969), 165–166, 192–193, 226; *Patria*, 3, 204.

[104] Alpay Pasinli, 'Pittakia ve Magnum Palatium-Büyük Saray Bölgesinde 2001 Yili Çalışmaları (Eski Sultanahmet Cezaevi Bahçesi)', *Müze Çalışmaları* 13 (2003): 5–9; Denker *et al.*, 'Former Sultanahmet Prison', 137–139; Asuman Denker, 'Excavations at the Great Palace', 17–18; Denker, 'Great Palace (Büyük Saray)', 25; Mamboury and Wiegand, *Kaiserpaläste*, 35–38.

[105] Mamboury and Wiegand, Kaiserpaläste, 26–33.

[106] *Book of Ceremonies*, 200, 213–216, 260, 270, 545, 809.

**Figure 14** The Ramp House in Akbiyik Cd. Wikimedia Commons.

terrace and the palace proper. We know that to transition between the two, one had to cross a bridge located south of the great *triklinos*. This would have served to cross over the 40 m long street found to the north of the Mamboury Ac2 group.[107] Kostenec suggested that the Ramp House (Ba) matched the staircase of St Christina, down which empresses descended to take a bath three days after their wedding night.[108] This assumption is supported by several lines of evidence. Firstly, the staircase is the first in the galleries leading outside the palace. Secondly, the ramp is associated with the apse of an important building, and we know that the staircase of St Christina was associated with the *triklinos* of the Ovaton. Finally, the itineraries suggest that this complex was located at an intermediate point along the eastern route, and the ruins effectively occupy a central position within the route of the galleries running from the Magnaura to the southern end of the Upper Palace (Figure 15).

---

[107] *Ibid.*, 155, 213–216, 545–547, 566–569.
[108] *Ibid.*, 214–215; Kostenec, 'Heart of the Empire', 21; other authors disagree and place the staircase further north, close to Mamboury A, Eugenia Bolognesi, 'The Great Palace Itineraries', *Araştırma Sonuçları Toplantıları* 26 (2006): 197–198, Westbrook, *Great Palace*, 204–211.

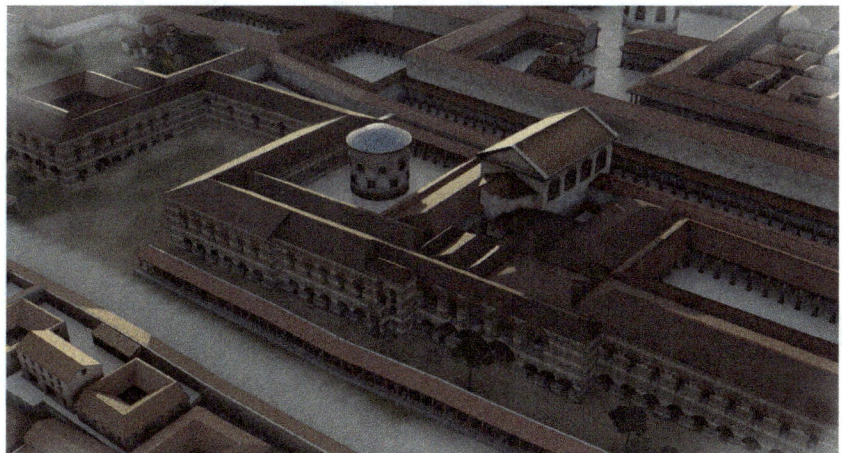

**Figure 15** View of the Ovaton and the Mamboury B complex. Author.

Following this reasoning, the polygonal apse (Bc) would correspond to the *triklinos* of the Ovaton. We know that in order to reach the staircase of St Christina, it was necessary to pass 'at the side of the Ovaton', and then 'behind the Ovaton', which aligns with the position of the apse, the adjacent galleries, and the ramp.[109] This hall, also known as the *triklinos* of the Dome or Troullos, was given its name due to its connection with the archive of the treasury, which, in accordance with the tradition of *skeuophylakia* (treasuries) had a centralised plan and was topped by a dome.[110] The building is attributed to either Constantine or Anastasius.[111] The *triklinos* of the Ovaton was primarily known for hosting the Sixth (680–681) and Quinisext (696) councils, after which they were known as Trullan Councils.[112] The building was still in use in the late twelfth century, as the wedding of Alexius II (r. 1180–1183) and Agnes of France (1180) was celebrated there.[113]

---

[109] *Book of Ceremonies*, 215–216.
[110] *Ibid.*, 215–216, 545, 567, 593; Isabella Baldini-Lippolis, 'Lo skeuophylakion nell'architettura protobizantina', in Isabella Baldini-Lippolis and Anna Lina Morelli (eds.), *Oro sacro: Aspetti religiosi ed economici da Atene a Bisanzio* (Bologna: Ante Quem, 2014), 123–238. The same applies to the Dome of the Eight columns within the Scholai.
[111] *Patria*, 1, 60; Symeon, *Chronicle*, 102, 5; *Georgius Monachus, Patrologiae Cursus Completus, Series Graeca* 110, edited by Jean Paul Migne (Paris: 1863), 765; *Ioannis Zonarae Epitomae historiarum, Corpus Scriptorum Historiae Byzantinae* 47–49, 3 vols., edited by Moritz E. Pinder and Theodor Büttner-Wobst (Bonn: 1897), vol. 3, 143.
[112] *Acta Conciliorum Oecumenicorum. Series secunda. Concilium Universale Constantinopolitanum Tertium*, edited by Rudolf Riedinger (Berlin: De Gruyter, 1990–1992).
[113] *William of Tyre: A History of Deeds Done Beyond the Sea*, 2 vols., translated and annotated by Emily A. Babcock and August C. Krey (New York: Columbia University Press, 1943), 22, 4.

### 3.9 The Peristyle of the Mosaics and the Consistorium

#### *3.9.1 Archaeological Remains*

Mamboury Da emerges from the slope at the southern end of the B structures, representing the southeastern corner of a recess formed by the galleries. This indicates that the galleries continued further southward. Two additional ensembles were documented to the southwest of these remains. Db, dated to the sixth century, was a cruciform chamber with a groined vault, featuring four small rectangular spaces between the arms of the cross. This was preceded to the west by an antechamber, built with earlier materials, possibly from the fifth century. Mamboury Dc, comprising several cisterns, was discovered 20 m to the south of the aforementioned structure.[114]

Since the beginning of the century, the Scottish magnate Sir David Russell and his spiritualist friend, Wellesley Tudor Pole, had been contemplating the possibility of excavating in the area, following a revelation during séances conducted by Russian monks exiled from the Revolution.[115] At last, in 1935, the excavation began under the direction of James Houston Baxter, a professor of church history at the University of Glasgow. Works revealed a peristyle paved with a magnificent mosaic displaying hunting scenes and the remains of a cruciform church. After the Second World War, in 1952, Sir David Talbot Rice led a second campaign, which unearthed the Apsed Hall overlooking the courtyard.

The peristyle boasted monumental dimensions of 65 × 55.5 m, while the hall measured 32 × 16.5 m. The Mamboury Db complex was adjacent to the hall on its northern side, while the cisterns in Dc were adjacent to it on the southern side. A street and a sequence of galleries divided this primary ensemble from a secondary one located north of the peristyle, notable for the remains of a cruciform church. A passageway ran along the western end of the peristyle, while an elongated hall was attached to the southern outer wall. The peristyle was situated above the southeastern edge of the terraces of the Upper Palace, with the *piano nobile* (main floor) at approximately 26 m.a.s.l. This meant that the earth beneath the site had been disturbed and originated from elsewhere, complicating the dating process. Nevertheless, it was determined that the filling must have occurred between 500 and 540.[116]

---

[114] Mamboury and Wiegand, *Kaiserpaläste*, 26–33.
[115] Mary Whitby, 'The Great Palace Dig: The Scottish Perspective', in Robin Cormack and Elizabeth Jeffreys (eds.), *Through the Looking Glass: Byzantium Through British Eyes* (London: Routledge, 2000), 45–66.
[116] *Great Palace: First Report*, 5.

**Figure 16** The northern portico of the peristyle of the mosaics in the late sixth century. Author.

One of the earliest elements of the ensemble was the Paved Way, a two-level brick viaduct that ran through the centre of the courtyard in an east–west direction, deviating slightly from its axis. The surface was paved with marble slabs. It is important to note that the viaduct always terminated in front of the foundations of the hall, suggesting that a significant building may have already stood at the eastern end of the courtyard in the earliest phases of the complex.[117] A fundamental structure for the study of the peristyle, and the next one in chronological order, is a cistern located beneath the southern portico. The structure was clearly older than this portico, as it was crossed by the latter's foundations. The bricks used in the construction of the structure bore stamps typical of the sixth century, featuring two lines of text or a cruciform shape, signed by a certain Gaius.[118]

The subsequent phase of construction pertains to the peristyle and the hall. The peristyle comprised four porticoed galleries. The initial entry to the complex was located at the northwestern extremity of the peristyle (Figure 16). The northern portico, aligned with the entrance, featured recesses with built-in marble benches. In the 1980s and 1990s, an Austrian team resumed excavations at the site. Works uncovered evidence suggesting that, despite sharing the same plan, two successive peristyles must have existed on the site. The first peristyle

---

[117] *Ibid.*, 5–6; *Great Palace: Second Report*, 10–15.  [118] *Great Palace: Second Report*, 15–17.

may have been decorated with a bichrome mosaic floor in black and white, while the second and final peristyle was embellished with the magnificent hunting-themed mosaics (Figures 20–23). The pottery discovered in the layer of debris between the two floors provided a *terminus post quem* for the mosaic peristyle, indicating that it was constructed after the year 475.[119] The hall also stood upon earlier buildings, as evidenced by a complex network of infrastructures with successive phases. Its foundations revealed that the structure was divided into an antechamber by a thick wall pierced by three arches. This vestibule led to the actual hall through three doors corresponding to the inferior arches. The presence of pillars under the apse indicated that the floor level in this area was higher than that of the rest of the chamber.[120]

The mosaic remained exposed for an extended period, resulting in damage that required repairs. The broken sections were subsequently filled in with *opus signinum* (Roman waterproof mortar). Later, the complex underwent significant transformations. The north and south porticoes were walled, and repurposed into long galleries, while the western one was eliminated. The mosaic was meticulously protected by the application of marble slabs, which ultimately ensured its preservation. The Paved Way regained its central position when a new main door was opened at the western end of the courtyard, aligned with the viaduct. The final intervention involved the walling of the recesses with benches in the northern portico. At some point in the late twelfth century, the site was subjected to extensive damage, as evidenced by the discovery of weaponry and armour in a context suggestive of violence and fire (Figure 17).[121]

### 3.9.2 Previous Datings and Identifications of the Site

Paradoxically, the discovery of the mosaic has presented a challenge in determining the date of the site, as numerous approaches have favoured the stylistic examination of the pavement over a strictly archaeological and topographic point of view. In this context, the narrative surrounding the date of the mosaic reflects the broader perception of Late Roman and Byzantine art. The assumption was that the more 'Classical' or 'Hellenistic' the features of an iconography, the earlier its date, and vice versa. Considerations such as the coexistence of diverse levels of artistic

---

[119] Werner Jobst, *Mosaikenforschung im Kaiserpaläste von Konstantinopel* (Vienna: Verlag der Österreichischen Akademie der Wissenschaften, 1992), 28–63; Werner Jobst, 'Archäologie und Denkmalpflege im Bereich des Großen Palastes von Konstantinopel', *Araştırma Sonuçları Toplantıları* 11 (1993): 9–15; Jobst *et al.*, *The Great Palace Mosaic*, 58–61.
[120] *Great Palace: Second Report*, 26–49.
[121] *Great Palace: First Report*, 8–9; *Great Palace: Second Report*, 6, 9, 12, 23.

**Figure 17** The peristyle of the mosaics before and after the reform that removed the porticoes. Author.

quality, disparities between centre and periphery, and the persistence of prestigious models in specific contexts, like the court, were overlooked.

For instance, in the initial excavation report, the analysis of hairstyles and clothing led researchers to propose a date around the year 410, despite this being at odds with the archaeological evidence. In any case, all such dating was based on the erroneous presumption that the site was the terrace of the Pharos.[122] The sixth century was only considered after stylistic comparisons were established

---
[122] *Great Palace: First Report*, 15–21, 91–97.

with Syrian mosaics.[123] While Talbot Rice placed a greater emphasis on archaeology, he still relied heavily on stylistic labels such as 'Medieval', 'Classical', 'Hellenistic' or even 'neo-Attic' to suggest a date between 450 and 500. This was the case even when the author explicitly suggested that the work was executed later.[124]

Victor Lazarev proposed a date in the mid sixth century, after comparing the mosaic with silver plates from the reigns of Justinian and his successors.[125] Following initial reservations, Mango and Irving Lavin also unequivocally pointed to the sixth century.[126] Some years later, Per J. Nordhagen sparked a new trend, suggesting a later date for the mosaic. According to him, the mosaic's style would reflect a revival imitating the sixth century, believed to have been introduced by Justinian II (r. 685–695 and 705–711) around the year 700. Accordingly, the hall would be identified with the *triklinos* of Justinian II.[127] The proposal was so successful that some authors even spoke of a 'Justinian II style'.[128]

Although stylistic analysis has never been entirely abandoned, the 1970s saw the emergence of some criticism based on iconography and archaeology. For example, John W. Hayes studied the pottery, establishing a temporal framework for the creation of the mosaic, which he dated between 520 and 540.[129] Anthony Cutler showed that the mosaic incorporated models from different periods and geographical contexts, invalidating the stylistic dating hypothesis.[130] Gisela Hellenkemper-Salies undertook a significant reassessment of both the archaeological data and the mosaic's style, which led her to conclude that works were likely completed around 475. Nevertheless, her arguments have since been superseded, and the value of her work is essentially

---

[123] Doro Levi, *Antioch Mosaic Pavements* (Princeton: Princeton University Press, 1947), 581, n.1.
[124] *Great Palace: Second Report*, 161, 166–167.
[125] Victor I. Lazarev, 'Фрески Кастельсеприо (К критике теории Вейцмана о «Македонском Ренессансе»)', *Византийский Временник* 7 (1953): 373.
[126] Mango and Irving Lavin, 'David Talbot Rice, ed., The Great Palace of the Byzantine Emperors, Edinburgh University Press, 1958', *The Art Bulletin* 42 (1969): 67–73.
[127] Per J. Nordhagen, 'The Mosaics of the Great Palace of the Byzantine Emperors', *Byzantinische Zeitschrift* 56, 1 (1963): 53–68.
[128] David H. Wright, 'The Shape of the Seventh Century in Byzantine Art', in *First Annual Byzantine Studies Conference Abstracts of Papers* (Cleveland: 1975), 9–28.
[129] John W. Hayes, *Late Roman Pottery: A Catalogue of Roman Fine Wares* (London: The British School at Rome, 1972), 418.
[130] Anthony Cutler, 'The Elephants of the Great Palace Mosaic', *Bulletin d'information de l'Association internationale pour l'étude de la mosaïque antique* 10 (1985): 125–131.

bibliographic.[131] During this time, Salvador Miranda, a Mexican architect, concluded that, in topographical terms, the peristyle should be identified with the *triklinos* Augousteus.[132]

James Trilling's approach stands as the most comprehensive contribution to the mosaic's style, which he links to North African examples. Nonetheless, his article draws heavily on an iconological reading, as he implies that the depictions of violence mirror emperor Heraclius's troubled soul.[133] Chuck Morss's readings focus on a purely stylistic analysis, demonstrating a clear link between the mosaic and Syrian and the Levantine examples dated to the mid sixth century.[134]

It has been previously noted that Austrian archaeologists dated the mosaic after 475. Furthermore, they expressed a preference for attributing it to Justinian.[135] Subsequently, several proposals have been put forward. Bolognesi suggested that we are dealing with a structure known as the Apsis, related to the Triconch complex built by Theophilus (r. 829–842).[136] This interpretation, but from an iconographic perspective, has been adapted by Gianclaudio Macchiarella, who dated the mosaic to the ninth century.[137] Kostenec, espousing Trilling's arguments, proposed that the ensemble was constructed by Heraclius to host the performances of the circus factions, and was subsequently transformed by Theophilus into a warehouse known as the Karianos.[138] Featherstone has suggested that we may be dealing with another of Theophilus's constructions, the Margarites.[139]

The interpretation that merits the most consideration, given its foundation on archaeological evidence, is that of Bardill. In accordance with Miranda's perspective, Bardill postulated that the Apsed Hall is the Augousteus. Despite it

---

[131] Gisela Hellenkemper-Salies, 'Die Datierung der Mosaiken im Großen Palast zu Konstantinopel', in Jean Pierre Darmon and Alain Rebourg (eds.), *La mosaïque gréco-romaine 4: IVe Colloque international pour l'étude de la mosaïque antique*, Trèves 8–14 août 1984 (Paris: Association internationale pour l'étude de la mosaïque antique, 1994), 273–308.

[132] Salvador Miranda, 'Étude sur le Palais Sacré de Constantinople: Le Walker Trust et le Palais de Daphnè', *Byzantinoslavica* 44 (1983): 41–49.

[133] James Trilling, 'The Soul of the Empire: Style and Meaning in the Mosaic Pavement of the Byzantine Imperial Palace in Constantinople', *Dumbarton Oaks Papers* 43 (1989): 27–72.

[134] Chuck Morss, 'The Family of the Great Palace Mosaic', *Byzantine Studies Conference Archives* (1998) [https://bsana.net/conference/archives/1998/abstracts_1998.php, retrieved 3 January 2021].

[135] Jobst, *Mosaikforschung*; Jobst, *The Great Palace Mosaic*.

[136] Bolognesi, 'Gran Palazzo', 227.

[137] Gianclaudio Macchiarella, 'Date and Patron(s) of the Floor Mosaic of the Great Palace of the Emperors: A New Approach', in Gianclaudio Macchiarella (ed.), *Alpaghian: Raccolta di scritti in onore di Adriano Alpago Novello* (Naples: ScriptWeb, 2005).

[138] Kostenec, 'Heart of the Empire', 15–18.

[139] Michael Featherstone, 'Theophilus's Margarites: The "Apsed Hall" of the Walker Trust?' in Silvia Pedone and Andrea Paribeni (eds.), *'Di Bisanzio dirai ciò che è passato, ciò che passa e che sarà': Scritti in onore di Alessandra Guiglia* (Rome: Bardi Edizioni, 2018), 173–186.

being a Constantinian building, the mosaic and the main structures should be dated to around the year 600.[140] He postulated that the Paved Way had two phases, the lower one corresponding to the 4th or 5th centuries, and the upper one to the sixth century, based on the different size of the bricks found in each of the arcades. With regard to the cistern beneath the southern portico, he demonstrated that it could be dated after 518 or 533, when the use of cruciform monograms was introduced. After considering the size of the bricks, the use of the dative case, and the presence of cruciform monograms, he believed that the cistern was built at the end of the sixth century, further delaying the date of the whole complex built above it at least to the early seventh century. However, he admitted that the ceramic materials present in the earth fill and beneath the porticoes do not preclude a date as early as the year 500. After coins of Justinian, Phocas (r. 602–610), and Constantine IV (r. 668–685) were found upon the removal of the western portico, he suggested a *terminus post quem* for the reform of the marble pavement around the year 700. When analysing the Apsed Hall, Bardill argued that he could only identify phases dating back to the beginning of the sixth century at the earliest. While he acknowledged a succession of constructive phases and reinforcements, the main phase should be dated around the year 600. Bardill's assessment was particularly influenced by the size of the materials and a stamp found on a brick utilised during a reinforcement phase, which is securely dated to either the years 583/584 or 598/599, corresponding to the reign of Maurice.[141]

### 3.9.3 Chronological Analysis of Stamped Bricks

The initial certainty that must be considered before dating the peristyle is that the earth fill took place, according to Bardill, as early as around the year 500. However, as demonstrated by Hayes, it is unlikely that it occurred later than the year 540. Prior to the final fill, the upper arcade of the Paved Way may have been exposed, forming a raised walkway. This interpretation, rather than the two proposed constructive phases, would explain the observed difference in brick sizes. The height of this pre-existing walkway would have determined the level at which the peristyle was constructed.

Bardill proposed that the cistern under the southern portico was built in the late sixth century. However, this is not likely if we consider that the cistern preceded the earth fill, which has a terminal date of 540. He based his dating on

---

[140] Jonathan Bardill, 'The Great Palace and the Walker Trust Excavations', *Journal of Roman Archaeology* 12 (1999): 217–230.
[141] Jonathan Bardill, *Brickstamps of Constantinople*, 2 vols. (Oxford: Oxford University Press, 2004), 136–142.

the size of the bricks, the cruciform stamps, and the presence of the dative case. Though it is accurate to state that the bricks decrease in size over the course of the sixth century, Bardill himself admitted that there is a significant deviation in the measurements and that these cannot be employed as an absolute criterion for dating.[142] He also acknowledged that the size may vary depending on the function and size of the building, as he pointed out when studying the fifth-century baths located near the Kalenderhane Mosque.[143] However, the cistern was undoubtedly constructed after 518 or 533, as evidenced by the presence of the cruciform monogram. Although most stamps on the bricks appear in the genitive case, the dative case is not a solid argument for supporting a later date either. Concerning the bricks stamped by Gaius (1364.1a and 1365.1a), Bardill's own classification places similar examples in constructions dating to the first half of the sixth century, such as St Polyeuctus, Hagia Sophia, Hagia Eirene, the Basilica Cistern, and the ruins of the Hospice of Sampson.[144] Consequently, it can be inferred that the cistern was constructed between the years 518 or 533, when the cruciform monograms first appear, and the 540s, as inferred from the earth fill.

An analysis of the bricks found in the peristyle yields similar conclusions. Bardill types 666, 785.1 c, 880.1a, 1257.1a, 1342.3b, 1342.8a, and 1344.1 c were notably prevalent in the walls of the peristyle and several drainage conduits. These types were also found in the cross-shaped church to the north, as well as in sixth-century contexts such as Mamboury A, B, and C. Outside the palace, this type is also found in St Polyeuctus, the reconstruction of Zeuxippos, Hagia Sophia, Hagia Eirene, repairs to the Balaban Ağa Mosque dating to the sixth century, and the north church of the Kalenderhane complex from the mid sixth century. During the renovation of the marble floor, stamps 619.1a and 620.1a were repurposed in a conduit. The same stamps were also found beneath the hall and in the southern cistern. This stamp features the abbreviation 'skri-', which may refer to the rank of *skriniarios* or *skribon*. If it refers to the latter, the brick must be dated after 545, when this position was first recorded.[145] Similar examples can be found in Zeuxippos, in interventions undertaken in the palace of Antiochus during the sixth century, and again in Kalenderhane, with a similar date.

Beneath the remnants of the western portico, a coin of Justinian was discovered. Initially, it was thought that this suggested the emperor's involvement in covering the mosaic, a view partially shared by Bardill, who proposed that the coin was deposited during this phase.[146] However, considering the chronology

---

[142] *Ibid.*, 102–106.   [143] *Ibid.*, 150.
[144] From now on, the stamps will be referenced according to Bardill's classification (*ibid.*).
[145] *Ibid.*, 144.   [146] *Great Palace: First Report*, 16; Bardill, *Brickstamps*, 142.

of the bricks and the stratum, which coincided with the boundary between the Late Roman level and subsequent renovations, it is more probable that the coin was deposited during the construction of the peristyle.[147]

Regarding the infrastructures of the hall, Bardill admitted that a significant building already stood there by the year 500, as evidenced by repairs dated to the early sixth century.[148] It can be reasonably assumed that the Paved Way led to that building. Two significant groups of stamped bricks were unearthed below the hall. The first, dating to the early sixth century, was believed by Bardill to be the result of a massive reuse of building materials. Conversely, the group contemporary to the construction of the hall would be later, dating to the end of the century. In this group, nine out of ten stamps were of the 'skri-' type.[149] Another significant brick bore a stamp dated to 583/584 or 598/599, during the reign of Maurice (231.1b). This brick might be the main reason behind Bardill's dating of the complex to the late sixth century. However, only one specimen was discovered, detached from one of the vaults, which suggests that it originated from a restoration. This view would be further reinforced if the brick was promptly placed in 583/584, as a violent earthquake occurred that year.[150]

In conclusion, in the fifth century there was already a significant complex standing in the location of the peristyle, judging by the Paved Way and the infrastructures of the Apsed Hall. The analysis of stamps from the peristyle and the hall suggests that the main constructive phase took place in the mid sixth century, as it is also inferred from the *terminus ante quem* of the earth fill around 540 and the apparition of the 'skri-'-type stamps, probably dated from 545 onwards. This chronology aligns with the finding of Justinian's coin and the dating of the bricks. It can thus be reasonably concluded that the primary construction phase of the complex occurred during the latter half of this emperor's reign.

### 3.9.4 The Consistorium and the Church of the Lord

It is this author's opinion that the archaeological site should be identified with the Consistorium. To support this identification, it is essential to elaborate on the features of the building. The Consistorium was the main audience hall of the palace in Late Antiquity, where courtiers conducted the *adoratio* or *proskynesis* (prostration or obeisance) and foreign ambassadors were received by the emperor. It was also the place where he dictated laws before his council, the consistory, which gave its name to the building.[151] The hall is first documented

---

[147] *Great Palace: First Report*, pl. 12, figure 1.   [148] Bardill, *Brickstamps*, 143.
[149] *Ibid.*, 144.   [150] Theophylact Simocates, *History*, 1, 12, 1.
[151] For the functions of the assembly, see Roland Delmaire, *Les institutions du Bas-Empire romain, de Constantin à Justinien I: Les institutions civiles palatines* (Paris: Éditions du Cerf and

as early as 467, when an embassy from the Western Emperor Anthemius (r. 467–472) was received there. It also played an important role during the proclamation of Leo I (r. 457–474), Anastasius, and Justin I (r. 518–527).[152] Despite its early importance, the Consistorium holds a marginal position in the *Book of Ceremonies*, as by the tenth century it had been replaced by the Magnaura and the Chrysotriklinos. Even its name was forgotten, becoming known as 'the hall where the baldachin stands and where the *magistroi* are appointed'.[153]

The position of the Consistorium and its connections with other elements of the complex can be reasonably ascertained through its neighbouring structures. It was the last significant hall along the eastern route. The Church of the Lord was situated north of the building, the *triklinos* of the *kandidatoi* standing exactly opposite the chapel. As previously stated, the latter was adjacent to the eastern side of the Tribunal.[154] This position rendered the site a crucial junction where the eastern and western itineraries converged. The Consistorium was also near the ancient baths and not far from the Covered Hippodrome. However, the connection with these structures ended following the construction of the Triconch.[155] In any case, these clarifications are crucial, as they reinstate the position of the Consistorium at the southernmost edge of the Upper Palace. On the other hand, the position of the Church of the Lord roughly corresponds to the cruciform church to the north.

The Consistorium was preceded by the Onopodion, an area of uncertain nature. Here, courtiers, coming from the Gold Hand, would customarily greet the emperor before proceeding into the hall. Our knowledge of the Onopodion is limited to the fact that access was gained through a bronze door covered with a veil that led onto a marble floor. This door was located exactly in front of the Consistorium. Additionally, a triple door of the Onopodion is referenced.[156] Scholars such as Berger and Kostenec speculated that this space likely took on a horseshoe shape, given its name, meaning donkey hoof.[157] Guilland, however, proposed that it might have been a gallery wide enough for a donkey to pass through.[158] Prior to entering the Consistorium, another enigmatic chamber, known as the Indians, is referenced.[159]

---

Éditions du CNRS, 1995), 29–46 and *Reallexikon für Antike und Christentum*, supplement 11 (Stuttgart: Anton Hiersemann, 2004), 'Consilium, Consistorium'.
[152] *Book of Ceremonies*, 395, 415–416, 418, 427–428.   [153] *Ibid.*, 573, 578, 584, 595.
[154] *Ibid.*, 11, 20, 32, 84, 99, 107, 130, 168–169, 230, 239, 251, 270, 545, 566–567, 578, 593–594.
[155] *Ibid.*, 239, 249–251, 422, 699–700.
[156] *Ibid.*, 72, 129–130, 136, 143, 163, 176, 181, 232, 234, 264.
[157] Kostenec, 'Heart of the Empire', 6–7.   [158] Guilland, *Études*, vol. 1, 86.
[159] *Book of Ceremonies*, 234, 236.

In the sixth century the Consistorium was preceded by a space or antechamber known as the Anticonsistorium.[160] From here, one accessed the hall known as the Grand Consistorium, through three ivory doors that were usually covered with veils.[161] The Consistorium featured a floor adorned with porphyry *omphalia*, indicating the position where ambassadors were to kneel before the emperor. At the far end of the chamber, above three porphyry steps, stood the baldachin of the imperial throne.[162] The Grand or Summer Consistorium was adjacent to the Small or Winter Consistorium, where courtiers would often dress following their promotions.[163]

The hall's most distinctive feature was the baldachin (Figure 18). Corippus, who chronicled an embassy during the reign of Justin II (r. 565–578), described it as a structure supported by four columns and topped with a hemispherical dome that symbolised the vault of Heaven. Each corner was surmounted by the figure of a winged victory, bearing a laurel wreath. The entire structure was crafted from gold and adorned with precious stones and purple silks.[164] Several accurate representations of the artefact have come down to us: in the two ivories featuring Ariadne, the empress is depicted beneath the baldachin. Four centuries later, during Basil I's reign (r. 867–886), it is found again in a manuscript of the *homilies* of St Gregory (fol. 239 r) (Figure 19). The only difference from Corippus's description is the replacement of victories with eagles holding wreaths.

The location of the Church of the Lord has already been outlined. However, it is worth noting that it was also identified as one of the main entrances to the palace, in this case, on its eastern flank.[165] According to the *Patria*, Constantine was the builder of the church.[166] The only information available regarding the structure is that it possessed bronze doors, a narthex, and a sanctuary.[167] The interior of the church was used to store the insignia of high-ranking members of the hierarchy, including the Caesar, as well as the *labara* (military pennants, often decorated with a Chi-Rho) and dragon standards of the guards.[168]

---

[160] *Ibid.*, 404, 407.   [161] *Ibid.*, 63, 73, 233–234, 405–407, 428.
[162] *Ibid.*, 10–11, 63, 73, 98, 130, 144, 163, 181, 192, 229, 232, 234, 394–395, 398, 405–407, 573.
[163] *Ibid.*, 144, 233, 235, 265, 398, 405–406.
[164] *In Laudem Iustini Augusti Minoris Libri IV*, translated by Averil Cameron (Bristol: The Athlone Press, 1976), 3, 191–203.
[165] *Book of Ceremonies*, 99, 557, 566–567, 635.   [166] *Patria*, 1, 60.
[167] *Book of Ceremonies*, 32, 84, 99, 107, 168–169.   [168] *Ibid.*, 641, 711–712.

**Figure 18** Interior of the Apsed Hall interpreted as the Consistorium. Author.

### 3.9.5 Identifying the Peristyle (I): Topographical Analysis

The site's immediate characteristics, including the triclinium-peristyle layout and the scale of the complex, indicate that we are facing one of the main *triklinoi* of the Upper Palace, that is, the Augousteus, the Nineteen Couches, the Hall of Justinian II, or the Consistorium. As previously stated, Miranda and Bardill already suggested the Augousteus. However, the identification does not seem feasible: its location does not correspond with the site, and its orientation probably does not either. Some recognisable annexes, such as the Octagon, are absent, and the chronology of materials does not correspond to the Constantinian period. Nordhagen opted to identify the complex with the *triklinos* of Justinian II. The location appears more suitable, as this hall abutted the southern terraces. Nevertheless, it did so from the western side, not far from the

**Figure 19** The baldachin of the Consistorium in the *Homilies of St. Gregory*, 2nd half of the ninth century. Paris, BNF, Par. gr. 510, fol. 239 r.

curved end of the Hippodrome. Moreover, the construction of the building occurred around the year 700, when the peristyle had already been in existence for at least a century. The Nineteen Couches can be dismissed with minimal consideration, as it had a north–south orientation and was adjacent to the Hippodrome. In contrast, the Consistorium shares several features with the complex. Firstly, topographic coincidences will be listed:

(a) North of the Consistorium stood the Church of the Lord, which also served as an eastern entrance to the palace. To the north of the peristyle, the remains of a church were discovered, situated near the recess between groups Mamboury B and D. Given the upward slope of the area, it is possible that this structure was linked to the aforementioned access to the imperial residence.

(b) The Consistorium was situated on the eastern flank of the Upper Palace, like the excavated structures.

(c) Prior to the construction of the Triconch, the Consistorium was positioned opposite the Covered Hippodrome and the baths, at the southernmost point of the upper terraces, much like the peristyle complex.

(d) The *Book of Ceremonies* places important elements to the north and west of the Consistorium, namely the Church of the Lord and the Onopodion. However, nothing is mentioned east or south. This leads to the conclusion that, similarly to the peristyle, the Consistorium was situated at the southeastern corner of the Upper Palace.

The morphology of the site and that of the Consistorium also exhibit significant parallels:

(a) In the sixth century, the Consistorium was preceded by the Anticonsistorium, where ambassadors sat while waiting to be granted entrance to the hall. Marble benches were discovered in the northern portico of the peristyle, aligned with the entrance to the courtyard.
(b) The Consistorium was accessed through three ivory doors. Their material suggests that they did not open directly to the outside but rather to an antechamber. Entrance to the main room of the apsidal hall was via a vestibule and three doors, as evidenced by the infrastructure.
(c) The Consistorium had a smaller adjoining chamber known as the Winter Consistorium, and the Apsed Hall had a northern extension labelled Mamboury Db.
(d) In the Consistorium, the throne stood upon a dais with three porphyry steps. In the hall, the area of the apse was raised above the rest of the chamber.

The Onopodion deserves special attention. It has been just suggested that the Anticonsistorium was the original peristyle, and there is evidence to infer that the Onopodion was its later designation. After the renovation, when the porticoes of the peristyle were removed, a door was opened at the western end of the courtyard, which led directly to the Apsed Hall via the Paved Way. The Onopodion, situated in front of the Consistorium, featured a bronze door opening onto a marble platform that led to the hall. The marble dais mentioned in the *Book of Ceremonies* is designated as *marmarinon poulpiton*, meaning marble pavement, and is likely to have referred to the marble slabs that covered the Paved Way. The name of this place may have originated from its purpose, as it is known that ambassadors frequently brought horses as gifts for the emperor, which were then brought into the Consistorium itself.[169] It is possible that the Paved Way was left intact in order to prevent damage to the mosaic when the animals were led into the hall.

The successive interventions that were identified during the excavation also help to elucidate the shifts in ritual that are observed in the *Book of Ceremonies*. In the sixth century, ambassadors would access the complex through the door on the western end of the northern gallery, then wait on the marble benches, and finally enter the hall through the eastern portico. It seems probable that they

---
[169] *Ibid.*, 405.

would leave by traversing the southern and western porticoes, eventually arriving back at the same door through which they had entered. In subsequent centuries, the *Book of Ceremonies* implies that the Onopodion was not exactly a portico, in accordance with the space resulting from the renovations.[170] Following these itineraries, the emperor would access the Onopodion through a door situated opposite the Consistorium, after crossing a marble platform, mirroring the complex's appearance following the removal of the porticoes and the opening of a new door aligned with the Paved Way.

### 3.9.6 Identifying the Peristyle (II): Chronological Analysis

It is necessary to ascertain whether the history of the Consistorium and related buildings aligns with that of the excavated site. The Paved Way is the oldest surviving element of the complex and likely dates back to the fifth century. It is possible that this coincides with the construction of the first Consistorium, which may have occurred during the Theodosian period. In any case, the Consistorium's existence by the year 467 is beyond any doubt.

During this phase, the area occupied by the complex must have been smaller, as the cistern built after 518 that was found beneath the southern portico was not aligned with any of its structures. The erection of the peristyle is believed to have occurred at the same time or shortly after the earth fill. This must have happened after the construction of the cistern but before the 540s. It is likely that the main phase, which featured the figurative mosaic, commenced around that date. The reference to the Consistorium's ivory doors, dating to the coronation of Justin I in 518, indicates that, in broad terms, the hall's morphology, with its triple entrance, predated the main phase and was maintained after subsequent renovations.[171] If we accept that Maurice's brick indicates a restoration, it can be concluded that the building was already finished and had undergone restoration works in the 580s. Finally, the reform that suppressed the porticoes is likely to have taken place in the late seventh century, as deduced from the *terminus* determined by a coin of Constantine IV. The complex was destroyed towards the end of the twelfth century or the beginning of the thirteenth century, possibly in connection with the sack of the city during the Fourth Crusade.

Considering this chronology, the candidates for the construction of the peristyle are Justinian, Justin II, and Tiberius II (r. 578–582). Given the length of Justinian's reign and the significant building initiatives he led as emperor, he is the most likely candidate for the construction of the peristyle. In addition to

---

[170] *Ibid.*, 161–162  [171] *Ibid.*, 428.

the coin discovered during the excavations, there are other indications that point to Justinian. As mentioned above, in 528 he undertook the renovation of the Kathisma. It is possible that this intervention coincided with the commencement of works in the Consistorium because, at the same time, laws were not issued in this hall of the Great Palace, as was customary, but in a different one at Iucundianae, in the Hebdomon.[172] It is also noteworthy that Justinian decreed that the senators should participate in the meetings of the consistory and relocated its sessions to the palace, which could have coincided with a renovation of the Consistorium.[173] If these assumptions are correct, the peristyle would have been constructed sometime in the 530–550s, coinciding with the earth fill, and prior to 547, 551, or 557, when the descriptions of several embassies already imply the configuration of the complex during the mosaic phase.[174] While no emperor is credited with the construction or renovation of the Consistorium, it is worth noting that, according to Procopius:

> practically the whole Palace is new, and, as I have said, was built by the emperor Justinian; but it is impossible to describe it in words and it must suffice for future generations to know that it happens to be entirely the work of this emperor.[175]

### 3.9.7 Identifying the Peristyle (III): The Meaning of the Mosaic

To understand the iconography of the mosaic, it is of the utmost importance to stress the identity of the complex. We are not dealing with the pavement of an aristocratic villa, a church, or a synagogue. Rather, we are facing the portico of an audience hall within the imperial palace. It thus becomes necessary to inquire whether the iconography of the mosaic lends support to the identification with the Consistorium. Indeed, the Consistorium is the sole edifice within the palace that can be related with potential allusions to the mosaic. The first and most significant of these is the reference to a space in front of the Consistorium, which the *Book of Ceremonies* refers to as the Indians.[176] It is evident that the mosaic incorporates numerous elements that would have been readily identifiable to its contemporaries as Indian, particularly in the northern portico, which

---

[172] Theodor Mommsen *et al.*, *Corpus iuris civilis*, 3 vols. (Berlin: Weidmann, 1888–1895), *Codex Iustinianus*, 1, 2, 22; 1, 14, 12; 2, 55, 4; 4, 1, 12; 4, 34, 11; 5, 12, 30; 5, 30, 5; 6, 4, 3; 5, 42, 30; 6, 61, 6; 7, 45, 13; 8, 53, 34; 9, 48, 20.
[173] Ibid., *Novellae*, 62; Ioannes Lydus. *On Powers or the Magistracies of the Roman State*, translated and edited by Anastasius C. Bandy (Philadelphia: American Philosophical Society, 1983), 2, 9; *Procopius, with an English Translation, Gothic War*, 7, 32, 43.
[174] *Book of Ceremonies*, 398–407.  [175] Procopius, *On Buildings*, 1, 10.
[176] *Book of Ceremonies*, 234, 236; it is very important to note that chapter 46 mentions court ranks that disappeared at the beginning of the eighth century. It is therefore very likely that the chapter was written before the covering of the mosaic, around the year 700.

**Figure 20** Peristyle of the mosaics: members of the factions hunting a tiger. Wikimedia Commons.

**Figure 21** Peristyle of the mosaics: a manticore. Wikimedia Commons.

is aligned with the main doorway and is the place where the benches are situated. The mosaic scenes can be classified in several groups, although there is considerable overlap between them, including hunting scenes and animal fights, which are presented either from a realistic (Figure 20) or mythological (Figure 21) point of view. There are numerous depictions of rural life and agricultural activities as well (Figure 22). Hippodrome-themed scenes are also depicted from a symbolic perspective, with children playing hoops around the *metae* (turning points of a circus) (Figure 23). References to the factions are

**Figure 22** Peristyle of the mosaics: bucolic scenes. Wikimedia Commons.

found throughout the mosaic, as is the case with the hunters dressed in their respective colours. Finally, a single triumphal scene has survived, depicting the arrival of the child Dionysus and his retinue or *thiasos*.

The Dionysian procession symbolises the arrival of the child-god in India, possibly in the mythical city of Nisa, which may be identified with the reclining woman, who is evidently a personification.[177] The *thiasos* is accompanied by local fauna, including a satyr, an elephant, and a white camel.[178] Additionally, the presence of other animals, such as lynxes, panthers, the enormous tiger at the entrance, and trained monkeys hunting birds, further reinforce the notion of an

---

[177] *Lexicon Iconographicum Mythologiae Classicae*, vol. 3 (Zurich: Artemis Verlag, 1986), 'Dionysos'; Robert Turcan, *Les sarcophages romains à représentations dionysiaques: Essai de chronologie et d'histoire religieuse* (Paris: De Boccard, 1966); Katherine Dunbabin, 'The Triumph of Dionysus on Mosaics in North Africa', *Papers of the British School at Rome* 39 (1979): 52–65; Pierre Schneider, *L'Éthiopie et l'Inde: Interférences et confusions aux extrémités du monde antique* (VIIIe siècle avant J.-C.–VIe siècle de notre ère) (Rome: École Française de Rome, 2004), 117–121, 127–128.

[178] Schneider, *L'Éthiopie et l'Inde*, 153–159; Lihi Habas, 'Camel Caravans and Trade in Exotic Animals in the Mosaics of the Desert Margin', in Leah di Segni (ed.), *Man Near a Roman Arch: Studies Presented to Prof. Yoram Tsafrir* (Jerusalem: Israel Exploration Society, 2009), 54–73.

**Figure 23** Peristyle of the mosaics: children playing hoops in the Hippodrome. Wikimedia Commons.

Indian setting.[179] Similarly, the depiction of fantastical creatures, including griffins and a manticore, which ancient sources consistently associate with India, further substantiate this hypothesis.[180] These creatures, along with the menacing monsters, collectively evoke a land as fantastical and threatening as the beasts themselves were perceived to be.[181] The portrayal of exotic creatures from distant lands alludes to the universal aspirations of the Roman Empire, which claimed the *dominium mundi*. This mosaic is not an isolated case; other examples, such as those at Villa del Casale or Mount Nebo, also exhibit this symbolism. In the Sicilian mosaic, the limits of the world are conveyed by the fauna. At the northern end of the portico stands the personification of Africa, surrounded by elephants and panthers. Hunters are depicted capturing the animals, which are later transported to Italy, located in the middle of the pavement. At the eastern end sits the personification of India, accompanied by a tiger and an elephant. In contrast to Africa, India was not particularly well known to the Romans. In order to evoke this sense of mystery, mythological animals such as a griffin and a phoenix were also incorporated beside the

---

[179] Schneider, *L'Éthiopie et l'Inde*, 169–171, Christophe Vendries, 'L'auceps, les gluaux et l'appeau: La ruse du chasseur d'oiseaux', in Jean Trinquier and Vendries (eds.), *Chasses antiques* (Rennes: Presses Universitaires de Rennes, 2009), 119–140.

[180] Schneider, *L'Éthiopie et l'Inde,* 190–193.

[181] Grant Parker, *The Making of Roman India* (Cambridge: Cambridge University Press, 2008), 78–80, 121–132.

personification.[182] In Mount Nebo, Indians and Persians, accompanied by exotic animals, represent the boundaries of the known world.[183] The Indian element was also adopted in the imperial *milieu*, combining its character of exotic refinement with its meaning of universality. This is exemplified by a silver *missorium* depicting a personification of India and by the Barberini Ivory, in which Persians and Indians, accompanied by exotic animals, present gifts to the emperor.[184]

However, the mosaic does not merely contain references to the remote and exotic ends of the world. Examples of scenes related to the Hippodrome can be observed, such as the one with children playing hoops. For Roman and Byzantine writers, this was an unmistakable symbol of cosmic order and social harmony.[185] The mosaic depicts children throughout, not only in the circus scene. This iconography may be related to a paternalistic attitude frequently observed in imperial discourse. The emperor was regarded as the *pater Patriae*, and his subjects were viewed as his children, for whose welfare he was responsible. In particular, Justinian employed this propagandistic device extensively. In other scenes, such as that of the mother suckling her child, the imagery may be understood as a more direct reference to Rome itself.[186]

Finally, we will analyse the georgic and hunting scenes and the *venationes* (animal hunts in the arena). This is where we find the second possible reference to the mosaic in written sources. In his eulogy to Justin II, Corippus used these themes to describe the reception of an Avar embassy in the Consistorium:

> [The emperor is] like a farsighted shepherd who has pastured bulls and woolly sheep in the grassy meadows over a long period, and knows all the names which he has given to the bulls; he rejoices that his dear flock is growing, he enters the pen, separates the weaker ones and brings together the lambs, calling them all by well-known names; when they hear his voice they

---

[182] Andrea Carandini *et al.*, *Filosofiana: La Villa de Piazza Armerina* (Palermo: Atlante, 1982), 194–230.

[183] Michele Piccirillo and Eugenio Alliata, *Mount Nebo: New Archaeological Excavations, 1967–1997*, 2 vols. (Jerusalem: Stadium Biblicum Franciscanum, 1998).

[184] Jocelyn M. C. Toynbee and Kenneth S. Painter, 'Silver Picture Plates of Late Antiquity: A.D. 300 to 700', *Archaeologia* 108 (1986): 39; Anthony Cutler, 'Barberiniana: Notes on the Making, Content, and Provenance of Louvre OA. 9063', in Anthony Cutler, *Late Antique and Byzantine Ivory Carving* (Aldershot: Ashgate Variorum, 1998), 329–339; Alicia Walker, *The Emperor and the World: Exotic Elements and the Imaging of Middle Byzantine Imperial Power, Ninth to Thirteenth Centuries C.E.* (Cambridge: Cambridge University Press, 2012), 7ff.

[185] Emily B. Lyle, 'The Circus as Cosmos', *Latomus* 43, 4 (1984): 827–841; Véronique Dasen, 'Hoops and Coming of Age in Greek and Roman Antiquity', in *Proceedings of the 8th International Toy Research Association World Conference* (July 2018) (Paris: Toy Research Association, 2019), 1–17.

[186] Cameron, *Procopius and the Sixth Century* (London: Routledge, 1985), 244–263.

follow and recognise their master, and baa into the air and greedily take the green grass which he has brought.[187]

The emperor is thus the good shepherd of his flock, his subjects, who by their obedience earn the favour of the ruler. In the context of the mosaic, these scenes represent the Roman people in an idealised manner. Conversely, violent scenes present the opposite situation:

> As Hyrcanian tigers when New Rome gives spectacles to its people, under the direction of their trainer do not roar with their usual savagery but enter, go all round the edge, and look up at the circus full of thousands of people, and by their great fear learn gentleness: they lay down their fury and are happy to wear the cruel chains, to come right into the middle, and they love in their pride the very fact that they are stared at. Their eyes range over the benches and the enthusiastic crowds and they lie down in adoration before the throne of the emperor.[188]

After this interpretation, the depiction of beasts being slain might point to all those, here specifically foreign peoples, who refuse to submit to imperial authority. It is deemed imperative that they acknowledge the supremacy of Rome; otherwise, they are doomed to be hunted like prey and paraded in the Hippodrome. The preceding passages are of significant importance, as they describe a reception in the Consistorium and bear a striking resemblance to several scenes in the northern portico, through which the ambassadors were required to pass before reaching the hall. These include the fight with the tiger just after crossing the threshold and, later, several pastoral scenes. It is worth emphasising the close relationship between the iconological interpretation of the mosaic presented here and the functions of the Consistorium, where the meetings of the emperor's privy council were held and foreign embassies were received. In conclusion, the pavement's iconography can be understood as an idealised representation of the Empire, as reflected in the bucolic and circus scenes. On the other hand, the hunting episodes represent the ominous fate awaiting traitors and external enemies. When considered alongside the Indian repertoire, these scenes symbolise the submission of the entire orb to imperial rule 'in such powerful vigour that under its control, exercised both at home and abroad, the whole world was subjected to the Roman yoke ... not only eastward and westward, but also laterally, to both bounds of the earth's circle'.[189]

---

[187] Corippus, *In Praise of Justin II*, 4, 198–209.   [188] *Ibid.*, 3, 244–255.
[189] *The Novels of Justinian*, translated and annotated by David J. D. Miller and Peter Sarris (Cambridge: Cambridge University Press, 2018), novel 62.

## 3.10 The Covered Hippodrome and the Skyla

The Covered Hippodrome was a courtyard of the palace, notable for its role as an access and nodal point between different areas of the imperial residence. The structure acquired its designation due to its resemblance to a circus and because its curved end, known as the hemicycle of the Skyla, was roofed.[190] The enclosure of the Skyla is thought to have been constructed during the reign of Tiberius II, who is credited with the creation of the Skyla Gate, which separated the covered area from the courtyard proper.[191] Later, Justinian II took advantage of this fact and transformed this space into the vestibule of his *triklinos*. The Scylitzes Matritensis contains a representation of the court in the miniature depicting the assassination of Leo V (fol. 26 v) (Figure 24).

The *Patria* attribute its construction to Constantine and assert that emperors used to leave the palace by chariot through this courtyard.[192] The attribution is consistent, as spaces with a similar layout have been documented in the Tetrarchic palaces of Milan and Sirmium, closely connected to the circuses of these cities.[193] This function also seems correct because the courtyard was used

**Figure 24** The Covered Hippodrome in the Scylitzes manuscript, second half of the twelfth century. Madrid, BNE, VITR/26/2, fol. 26v.

---

[190] *Book of Ceremonies*, 269, 272–274.  [191] Genesius, *On the Reigns of Emperors*, 4, 9.
[192] *Patria*, 1, 60 and 2, 129.
[193] Vladislav Popović and Edward L. Ochsenschlager, 'Der spätkaiserzeitliche Hippodrom in Sirmium', *Germania* 54, 1 (1976): 163–165; Alberto de Capitani D'Arzago, *Il Circo Romano: Ricerche della Commissione per la forma urbis Mediolani* (Milan: Ceschina, 1939), 7, 55ff.

as a stable.[194] For this reason, it was also known as Kaballarios.[195] As previously stated, the Covered Hippodrome was an important junction, connecting the Upper and Lower Palaces via the Galleries of Daphne and the *triklinos* of Justinian II, respectively. The baths of the Constantinian residence, the Thermastra, were also immediately adjacent to the courtyard.[196] Besides, the complex comprised two major entrances to the palace from the city: the Karea Gate, opening directly onto the arena of the circus after passing under the Kathisma, and the Galleries of Marcian, which ran parallel to the *sphendone* (curved end of a Roman circus).[197] Along these galleries, under the infrastructure of the Hippodrome, the Palatine Court of Justice known as the Veil and its related archives were located. This complex dedicated to the administration of justice is often referred to as *asekreteia*.[198] Due to its strategic location within the palace, the Covered Hippodrome housed a garrison of soldiers and was therefore known as Spatharikion (Figure 25).[199]

**Figure 25** The Covered Hippodrome and the Skyla. Author.

---

[194] *Book of Ceremonies*, 699–701; Nicholas Mesarites, *Coup of John the Fat*, 11, 28.
[195] *Book of Ceremonies*, 6, 557, 616; *Patria*, 1, 60.   [196] *Book of Ceremonies*, 699.
[197] *Ibid.*, 122; *Vita Basilii*, 88, 90. The *Book of Ceremonies*, 337 mentions an otherwise unknown Hippodrome of St Sergius in the vicinity of the homonymous church and the Galleries of Marcian. It might be tempting to identify it with a curved wall attached to the *sphendone* of the Hippodrome, as seen in Onufrio Panvinio's engraving from *De ludis circensibus*.
[198] John the Lydian, *The magistracies*, 3, 19; *Les listes de préséance byzantines des IXe et Xe siècles*, introduction, text, translation, and commentary by Nikolaos Oikonomides (Paris: CNRS, 1972), 322–323.
[199] *Book of Ceremonies*, 96, 125, 157, 718.

## 3.11 Additions to the Upper Palace

### 3.11.1 The Triklinos of Justinian II

Following the interventions undertaken during the reign of Justinian, the area occupied by the Upper Palace was almost filled. The only remaining space was to the south, at the edge of the terraces at 26 m.a.s.l., and it was there where subsequent extensions were carried out.

The first significant expansion of the palace in over a hundred years was undertaken by Justinian II, who, between 692 and 694, built the hall bearing his name, the two *phialai* (ritual fountains) of the factions, the walls of the Lower Palace and, according to the *Patria*, also the *triklinos* Lausiakos.[200] The main function of Justinian's *triklinos* was to host imperial banquets. Additionally, it served as a gathering point for courtiers, who awaited there for the start of the daily processions after having entered the palace through the Covered Hippodrome. Thus, the *triklinos* of Justinian was also known as the procession hall.[201] The western end of the hall led directly to the Skyla through a door.[202] At the southeastern end, another door opened onto two distinct routes: the staircase leading down to the Lower Palace and the balcony overlooking the fountain of the green faction, located in the lower level as well.[203] This indicates that the hall rose almost on the edge of the terrace.[204] The location of the *triklinos* can also be determined with relative certainty, as several sources place it near a cistern likely to be identified with the one beneath Nakilbent Sk.[205]

The *triklinos* was decorated with gold mosaics and polychrome marbles, including several *omphalia*.[206] The emperor's table occupied a special place at the eastern end of the hall, separated from the main space by a railing.[207] The *triklinos* of Justinian II retained its splendour until 1295, when a gust of wind blew the roof off. In 1345 the remains of the building were still used as a prison.[208]

### 3.11.2 The Pavilions of Theophilus and Basil I

The next enlargement took place during the reign of Theophilus, who built several pavilions, a number of which stood within the Upper Palace. These

---

[200] Theophanes, *Chronicle*, AM 6186; *Patria*, 3, 130.  [201] *Book of Ceremonies*, 161, 286.
[202] Ibid., 123, 293, 523–524.  [203] Ibid., 89, 286, 288–289.
[204] Kostenec, 'Heart of the Empire', 14.
[205] *Vita Basilii*, 92; Scylitzes, *Synopsis of History*, Bas1, 41; Mamboury and Wiegand, *Kaisepaläste*, 47–49.
[206] Theophanes Continuatus 3, 44; *Book of Ceremonies*, 86–87, 286.
[207] Ibid., 287–288, 595–596, 775.
[208] *Georges Pachymérès. Relations historiques, Corpus Fontium Historiae Byzantinae* 24, 5 vols., edited and translated by Albert Failler and Vitalien Laurent (Paris: Les Belles Lettres, 1984–2000), 8, 15; *Ioannis Cantacuzeni Eximperatoris Historiarum Libri IV, Corpus Scriptorum Historiae Byzantinae* 5–7, 3 vols., edited by Ludwig Schopen (Bonn: 1828–1832), 3, 87.

**Figure 26** The Triconch of Theophilus and the Sigma. Author.

buildings were described in detail by the Continuator of Theophanes, who also listed them in order, in accordance with the itineraries from the *Book of Ceremonies*.[209]

Close to the entrance of the palace by the Church of the Lord stood the Karianos, so named due to the presence of steps carved in Carian Marble. It was initially used by Theophilus as a winter dormitory and, later, as a dressing room.[210] The next complex on the itinerary was the Sigma-Triconch (Figure 26). As its name suggests, the Triconch had three apses, one facing east and the other two facing north and south. The eastern apse was raised and supported by four porphyry columns.[211] It was constructed above a foundation with a similar configuration, although the apses faced west, south, and east. The northern space was referred to as the Mysterion because the echo made it impossible to share a secret there. To the west, through tripartite entrances with bronze and silver doors, both levels opened onto the portico of the Sigma, named after its semicircular plan. The superior level was supported by fifteen columns made of Docimian marble. In the centre, a canopy supported by four columns of Thessalian marble stood above the imperial throne. The lower level was supported by nineteen marble columns. To the west lay a courtyard paved with marble slabs. Centrally positioned within this space was a fountain featuring a silver rim and a pinecone-shaped spout. Two additional lion-headed spouts on either side enabled the flooding of the courtyard. Some scholars have

---

[209] *Theophanes Continuatus* 3, 42–43.   [210] *Book of Ceremonies*, 582, 592.
[211] Ibid., 298, 300.

compared these features to the *saradib*, cryptoporticoes cooled by pools, typical of Islamic architecture, which may have inspired Theophilus.[212] Other examples of two-storey triconch buildings opening onto courtyards can be found in the Levant, including the Palace of Trajan at Bosra and Qasr ibn-Wardan, dating to the sixth century. The Umayyads seem to have implemented a similar type at Qasr al-Qastal.[213] Thus, the Islamic origin of the Sigma complex remains a matter of debate.

The western end of the courtyard was enclosed by several buildings. At the centre, a staircase of Proconnesian marble led to the upper levels. Above the staircase was an arch supported by two columns known as the Apsis, a term often used by the *Book of Ceremonies* to refer to the whole complex. The chamber on the lower level was called Pyxites, while the corresponding room on the superior level served as a dormitory for the palace clergy. A chapel dedicated to St John also stood within this complex.[214] The cornices surrounding the courtyard were decorated with verses written by courtly poets. Further west the ensemble was connected to the Thermastra and from there to the Covered Hippodrome. To the north it communicated with the Galleries of Daphne, and to the northeast with the Galleries of the Church of the Lord. Meanwhile, the galleries departing from its southern side led to the Lower Palace.[215]

The following pavilion was, somewhat ironically, named Eros, despite its actual purpose as an armoury. It was therefore decorated with images of panoply. According to the Continuator's itinerary, this structure was located to the east of the Triconch. It must have been one of the southernmost buildings of the Upper Palace, since, as we have seen, the passageways that ran along its eastern side were known as the Galleries of Eros. For this reason, it is tempting to identify it with a hall attached to the southern portico of the mosaic peristyle, as it stands at the very end of the eastern galleries.[216] South of the Eros stood the Margarites, that is, the Pearl. Theophilus used this pavilion as a summer

---

[212] Nigel Westbrook, 'Exchange of Palatine Architectural Motifs between Byzantium, Persia and the Caliphate', in Danijel Dzino and Ken Parry (eds.), *Byzantium, its Neighbours and its Cultures* (Leiden: Brill, 2017), 129–153.

[213] Pauline Piraud-Fournet, 'Le Palais de Trajan à Bosra: Présentation et hypothèses d'identification', *Syria* 80 (2003): 5–40; Arnau Perich Roca, 'El palacio de Qasr ibn Wardan (Siria) y la evolución de la tipología palacial bizantina (siglos VI–XV)', *Revista d'arqueologia de Ponent* 23 (2013): 45–74; Patricia Carlier, 'Recherches archaeologiques au Château de Qastal (Jordanie)', *Annual of the Department of Antiquities of Jordan* 28 (1984): 343–383.

[214] *Book of Ceremonies*, 297–298, 309–310.

[215] *Ibid.*, 84, 107, 169, 303–304, 574, 584–585, 601–602, 605. For the southern connections, see Section 3.1.2.

[216] *Great Palace: First Report*, 12–13.

bedroom, as opposed to the Karianos. The Margarites comprised two parts. The western structure was supported by eight pink marble columns and decorated with mosaics of animals and fruit trees. The floor was paved with Proconnesian marble and *sectilia* (inlaid polychrome marble floors). The dormitory itself, located to the east, was supported by four columns. Two porches were located on the exterior of the structure, one to the east and one to the south, each supported by four green marble columns. The position of these porches is significant, as it implies that the building must have stood at the southeastern corner of the upper terraces.

A few decades later, Basil I undertook the last expansion of the Great Palace. He constructed additional buildings at the southern edge of the terraces, overlooking the halls of the Lower Palace. We only know that one was referred to as the Pyramids due to the shape of its roof, while another was called Aetos, Eagle, because of its considerable height. The latter was also related to a chapel of the Theotokos.[217]

### 3.12 Connections between the Upper and Lower Palaces

The southern end of the terraces of the Upper Palace stood at approximately 26 m.a.s.l., above infrastructures and vaulted chambers at about 21 m.a.s.l. The subterranean chambers supporting the edge of the terrace were probably considered part of the Thermastra due to the presence of an underground level associated with the hypocaust.[218] Through this intermediate floor, it was possible to descend in two directions to the main level of the Lower Palace at 16 m.a.s.l. The first descent, to the west, led to the *triklinos* Lausiakos, while the second provided access to the *diaitarikion*, a sentry post and office of the *papias*, keyholder of the palace.[219] As we shall see, these entrances coincide with the two main staircases that connected the upper and lower precincts, and thus it is quite likely that they were connected to them in some way.

The western staircase connected the *triklinos* of Justinian II and the Lausiakos.[220] Galleries departing from the Triconch also led to this staircase, after passing through the *eidikon*, an imperial storeroom.[221] The so-called Galleries of the Forty Martyrs also extended from the Triconch, in this case leading to the eastern staircase, which descended directly to the Pantheon, the northern vestibule of the Chrysotriklinos.[222] The sources refer to a chapel

---

[217] *Vita Basilii*, 90.   [218] Guilland, *Études*, vol. 1, 120–129.
[219] *Book of Ceremonies*, 289, 340.
[220] *Ibid.*, 86, 89, 114, 122, 171–174, 285–286, 288, 296, 442, 518, 523, 580, 585–586, 588, 595–596.
[221] *Ibid.*, 91, 169, 174–175, 180, 264, 297, 519.
[222] *Ibid.*, 71–72, 85, 107, 129, 169, 180, 261, 298, 304, 310, 348, 545, 567.

## The Great Palace

dedicated to St Michael near the edge of the terrace, in connection with this staircase.[223] It is possible that it was incorporated into the staircase itself, as was the oratory at the top of the Ramp House.

It is necessary to address a problem related to the eastern staircase and the so-called Ivory Door before concluding this section. Determining the position of this access is important in order to clarify the topography of the area and to situate historical events, such as the assassination of Emperor Leo V. However, there are two opposing traditions: one situates the Ivory Door and the magnicide next to the chapel of St Stephen in Daphne, while the other places it near the Church of the Pharos, in connection with the eastern staircase leading down to the Lower Palace. Guilland, followed by most scholars, recognised the problem and leaned towards the first option, as no sources seemed to point to the Lower Palace.[224] However, Genesius does explicitly mention the Church of the Pharos.[225] This reference corroborates the second account and aligns more closely with the indications of the *Book of Ceremonies*, which mentions the Ivory Door in connection with the vestibule of the Chrysotriklinos, the afore-mentioned Pantheon.[226] In the vicinity was the Ivory Prison, named after the door.[227] This fact reinforces the proposed location for the access, as the prison was likely part of the *diaitarikion*, the *papias*' office, which, as previously noted, was related to the Chrysotriklinos staircase and the Pharos Terrace.

### 4 The Lower Palace

Bolognesi proposed that the Lower Palace comprised three descending terraces. The first of these was the platform known as the Chrysotriklinos or Pharos Terrace, which was located at 16 m.a.s.l. However, it has not been reliably documented by archaeology. The second terrace, situated at 11 m.a.s.l., provided support for the *piano nobile* of the maritime façade, namely the group of buildings known as the Boukoleon, and has been documented. Finally, at 6 m.a.s.l., Bolognesi posited the existence of a third terrace, comprising the infrastructure of the preceding level and offering direct access to the sea from the palatine harbour.[228]

---

[223] Jan Kostenec, 'Observations on the Great Palace at Constantinople: The Sanctuaries of the Archangel Michael, the Daphne Palace, and the Magnaura', *Reading Medieval Studies* 31 (2005): 27–35.

[224] Rodolphe Guilland, 'Études sur le Grand palais de Constantinople: La Porte d'Ivoire; ἡ ἐλεφαντίνη πύλη', *Byzantion* 34, 2 (1964): 329–346.

[225] Genesius, *On the Reigns of Emperors*, 1, 16.   [226] *Book of Ceremonies*, 518, 600.

[227] Scylitzes, *Synopsis of History*, Const9, 21; *The Alexiad*, translated by Peter Frankopan and Edgar R. A. Sewter (London: Penguin, 2009), 14, 9; *John Kinnamos. Deeds of John and Manuel Comnenus*, translated by Charles M. Brand (New York: Columbia University Press, 1976), 7, 2.

[228] Bolognesi, 'The Great Palace', 9–10.

To the west, the first notable structure was the *triklinos* Lausiakos, which, as previously stated, was situated adjacent to one of the staircases descending from the Upper Palace. The eastern side of the hall communicated with a portico known as the Tripeton or Horologion, due to the presence of a clock. In turn, the eastern side of the Tripeton also led to the Chrysotriklinos, which was the undisputed heart of the Lower Palace. In the tenth century, this space was used for both imperial audiences and banquets. The Chrysotriklinos had several annexes, such as the Pantheon, which provided access to the eastern staircase, and the Chapel of St Theodore. To the east of the Golden Hall extended the Pharos Terrace, which was overlooked by several churches, including those of St Demetrios and the Theotokos. To the south, the imperial apartments were also attached to the Chrysotriklinos. Finally, to the southwest, an open area was covered with gardens, pavilions, and chapels. At the end of the tenth century, Nicephorus Phocas surrounded the complex with walls. Beyond the eastern boundary of these walls stood the Nea Ekklesia, built by Basil I, and the polo field, known as the Tzykanisterion.

The maritime façade, or Boukoleon, was divided in two sections. The western part, now destroyed, was notable for a balcony with marble lions, while the eastern part, popularly known as the House of Justinian, had a terrace overlooking the imperial docks below. From there, access to the palace could be gained via the monumental staircase located between the two sections of the façade (Figure 27).

### 4.1 The Origin of the Lower Palace

The Lower Palace has its origins in a series of aristocratic residences that were situated along the banks of the Marmara. The most notable of these was the Palace of Hormisdas, constructed by Constantine for the brother of the Persian emperor Shapur II (r. 309–379). Even at this early stage, the complex already had direct access to the sea via a small harbour.[229] During the reign of Theodosius II (r. 408–450), the *Notitia Urbis Constantinopolitanae* mentions several residences owned by imperial women. Thus, we have records of the *domus* of Marina and Galla Placidia, and another residence inhabited by the latter's mother, known as the *palatium placidianum*.[230] These palaces lay along

---

[229] *Zosime. Histoire nouvelle*, 3 vols., edition and translation by François Paschoud (Paris: Les Belles Lettres, 1971–1989), 2, 27; *Patria*, 3, 39.

[230] *The Notitia Urbis Constantinopolitanae*, translated by John Matthews, in Lucy Grig and Galvin Kelly (eds.), *Two Romes: Rome and Constantinople in Late Antiquity* (Oxford: Oxford University Press, 2012), 230. In fact, several of these residences had occupied an earlier house, known as the domus of Flavius Ablabius, consul in the time of Constantine, Kostenec, 'Heart of the Empire', 25.

**Figure 27** View of the Lower Palace. Author.

the shore, extending from the present-day Kalyon Hotel to the site later occupied by the Church of St Sergius and Bacchus.

During the reign of his uncle Justin, Justinian resided in the Palace of Hormisdas, which by that time had probably incorporated the noble houses of the Theodosian period. Procopius highlights the splendour of this residence, which Justinian renovated and connected to the Great Palace.[231] One of the main reasons for this renovation was a fire that took place in 548. After the conflagration, the emperor maintained the palatial status of the eastern section of the complex but donated a significant part to the monastery of Hormisdas.[232] From the reign of Justinian onwards, there is evidence that emperors were moving southwards, closer to the sea. However, in logistical terms, the Palace of Hormisdas continued to be considered a separate complex until the 690s, when specific offices associated with it disappeared definitively.[233]

Nevertheless, it seems that some of its most important elements predate Justinian's reign. For example, the *Patria* attribute the founding of the Boukoleon and the Tzykanisterion to Theodosius II, and place the assassination attempt of his favourite, Paulinus, in the staircase of the Pantheon.[234] The Tzykanisterion, known as *lusorium* (recreational space), certainly existed during the reign of this emperor, and he is also credited with the renovation of the sea walls, which could point to the Boukoleon.[235] In this regard, the *Patria* might be recalling early interventions, while reflecting the architectural background and toponymy from a much later period. The Lausiakos hall, traditionally attributed to Justinian II, may in fact date back to the early fifth century, as evidenced by its name, which may be derived from the eunuch Lausus.[236] This dynamic is even observed in the Chrysotriklinos. Many sources attribute its construction to Justin I, Justin II, or Tiberius II.[237] However, as noted by Bologesni, it is certain that the building was already in existence in 532, when a synod held in the Palace of Hormisdas is described as happening 'in...eptaconcho triclinio'.[238] The *Patria* ascribe the construction of the edifice to Marcian (r. 450–457).[239] It is possible that he was the actual builder, since we know that he had constructed some galleries not far from there, near the Covered Hippodrome.

---

[231] Procopius, *On Buildings*, 1, 4; *Patria*, 3, 39.
[232] *John of Ephesus. Lifes of the Eastern Saints (II), Patrologia Orientalis* 18, Syriac text edited and translated by Edmund W. Brooks (Paris: Firmin Didot, 1924), 683–684.
[233] Kostenec, 'Heart of the Empire', 27. [234] *Patria*, 3, 29, 126, 146.
[235] *Notitia Urbis Constantinopolitanae*, 230; *Chronicon Paschale*, AD 439.
[236] *Patria*, 3, 130.
[237] Kostenec, 'Chrysotriklinos', in *Encyclopaedia of the Hellenic World* [http://constantinople.ehw.gr/forms/fLemmaBodyExtended.aspx?lemmaID=12440, retrieved 3 January 2021].]
[238] Bolognesi, 'Gran Palazzo', 236. [239] *Patria*, 3, 126.

In summary, in contrast to other sections of the palace, such as the Constantinian Daphne, the Lower Palace was not the outcome of a unified, centralised initiative. The formation of the complex was the consequence of the agglomeration of several aristocratic residences from the 4th, 5<sup>th</sup>, and 6th centuries, whose main buildings were preserved at all costs. In addition to topographical proximity and utilitarian criteria, the aristocratic pedigree of these domus and the prestige ascribed by the Byzantines to Late Antique monuments must have played an important role in this process.[240]

## 4.2 The *Triklinos* Lausiakos

As previously noted, the *Patria* associate this chamber with Justinian II. Nevertheless, the name of the hall may suggest an earlier origin, perhaps in the fifth century. The Lausiakos was frequently traversed by processions crossing the Lower Palace, yet its precise function remained ambiguous. It appears that it served as a monumental antechamber for the Chrysotriklinos. As previously stated, both this *triklinos* and that of Justinian II were situated in proximity to the Nakilbent cistern.

There is no evidence regarding the layout of the hall; however, the arrangement of the courtiers in rows on either side points to a rectangular plan.[241] Emperor Theophilus ordered the Lausiakos to be decorated with mosaics, and the roof was replaced with the coffering of the palace of the usurper Basiliscus (r. 475–476).[242] The *triklinos* is depicted in the Madrid Scylitzes as the setting for the torture of the Graptoi, presenting it as a rectangular building with a gabled roof (fol. 51 v). The Lausiakos had several gates and annexes. To the east, a bronze door covered by an arch led to the portico of the Horologion.[243] The kitchens of the Lower Palace were also attached to the Lausiakos and could be accessed directly through another bronze door.[244] Additionally, the southern side of the edifice was adjacent to the chapel of St Basil.[245] Finally, a door, which must have been situated on the north side, led to the Thermastra.[246] Along one side of the *triklinos* was a garden, which probably coincided with the location of the fountain of the greens.[247]

---

[240] As noted by Paul Magdalino in several articles, the most recent of which is 'Modes of Reconstruction in Byzantine Constantinople', in Emmanuelle Capet *et al.* (eds.), *Reconstruire les villes: Modes, motifs et récits* (Turnhout: Brepols, 2019), 255–267.
[241] *Book of Ceremonies*, 86, 175, 286, 297, 530.   [242] *Theophanes Continuatus* 3, 44.
[243] *Book of Ceremonies*, 260, 286, 518, 605; *Theophanes Continuatus* 6, 439.
[244] *Book of Ceremonies*, 519   [245] *Ibid.*, 137, 523, 539, 550, 559.   [246] *Ibid.*, 340.
[247] *Theophanes Continuatus* 3, 14; Scylitzes, *Synopsis of History*, Theoph. 10.

## 4.3 The Portico of the Horologion

The portico of the Horologion lay between the Lausiakos and the Chrysotriklinos.[248] The main function of this courtyard was to serve as a waiting room for the courtiers before entrance was allowed to the receptions and banquets held in the Golden Hall. Despite its designation, the clock that gave its name to the portico is only mentioned a couple of times.[249] Although it has been assumed that it was a sundial, it is possible that the *horologion* was in fact a mechanical clock, as the corps of the *horologioi*, experts in the operation of clocks, served within the palace.[250] It is also possible that it was associated with the watchtower system devised by Leo the Mathematician to warn of Arab attacks from Cilicia, which resulted in the installation of a clock located in the palace.[251]

Although usually thought of as separate spaces, Featherstone realised that the portico of the Horologion and the place called Tripeton were actually one and the same.[252] However, the origin of its name is obscure. Considering its etymology, it could refer to a portico covered only on three sides, but it may also allude to the ritual that awaited courtiers entering the Chrysotriklinos, who had to kneel three times before the emperor.

## 4.4 The Chrysotriklinos

As mentioned above, the Chrysotriklinos was the centre of the Lower Palace, and served as an audience and banqueting hall. It has also been suggested that, despite repeated attributions to sixth-century emperors, the building is likely to have been constructed at least a century earlier, possibly during the reign of Marcian. In any case, the building is mentioned as late as the fourteenth century.[253]

Due to its prominent role, the Chrysotriklinos is one of the best-known buildings within the palace. The floor plan of the hall was octagonal. Each of the eight sides had an apse, except for the western side, which led to the Horologion and was covered by a barrel vault. With the exception of the eastern conch above the throne, all the vaults were covered with veils. A large cornice

---

[248] *Book of Ceremonies*, 91, 119, 123, 518, 526–527, 529, 580, 585–586, 605, 618, 622, 625.
[249] *Ibid.*, 91, 622.   [250] *Ibid.*, 724.
[251] *Symeonis Magistri Annales, Corpus Scriptorum Historiae Byzantinae* 45, edited by Immanuel Bekker (Bonn: 1838), 681–682; *Theophanes Continuatus* 4, 35; see Philip Pattenden, 'The Byzantine Early Warning System', *Byzantion* 53, 1 (1983): 258–299.
[252] Michael Featherstone, 'The Chrysotriklinos as Seen Through De Cerimoniis', in Lars M. Hoffmann and Monchizadeh, Anuscha (eds.), *Zwischen Polis, Provinz und Peripherie: Beiträge zur byzantinischen Geschichte und Kultur* (Wiesbaden: Harrassowitz Verlag, 2005), 836; *Book of Ceremonies*, 92.
[253] Pachymeres, *Relations historiques*, 10, 36.

**Figure 28** The Chrysotriklinos in the Scylitzes manuscript, second half of the twelfth century. Madrid, BNE, VITR/26/2, fol. 14 r.

ran along the top of the vaults. Above it rose the drum, with a large window on each of its eight sides. The building was covered by a ribbed dome of sixteen segments, each pierced by a window.[254] The miniaturist of the Scylitzes Matritensis was well informed about the architecture of the Chrysotriklinos, which he depicted as a cylinder-shaped building crowned by a dome (fol. 14 r) (Figure 28).

The features listed above reflect a striking duality. The lower part is almost identical to Late Roman examples of centralised halls, such as the so-called Temple of Minerva Medica in Rome or the Octagon of the Palace of Galerius in Thessaloniki.[255] Conversely, the dome, probably supported by eight pendentives, ribbed and pierced with windows, is typical of Justinianic architecture, Hagia Sophia being the most remarkable example. This may explain the confusion of the sources regarding the construction of the building. The hall could date back to the fifth century or even to the foundation of the House of Hormisdas in the fourth century. However, the dome may have been destroyed by an earthquake or fire, later repaired by Justin II following new architectural trends, and then decorated by Tiberius II.[256]

---

[254] Featherstone, 'The Chrysotriklinos', 833–840.
[255] Andrea A. Biasci, 'Il padiglione del 'Tempio di Minerva Medica' a Roma: Struttura, tecniche di costruzione e particolari inediti', *Science and Technology for Cultural Heritage* 9 (2000): 1–22; Marianna Karamberi, 'Ο ρολός του Οκταγώνου στο Γαλεριανού συγκρότημα και η σχέση του με το μεγάλο περιστύλιο', *Αρχαιολογικά Ανάλεκτα εξ Αθηνών* 23–28 (1990–1996): 116–128.
[256] Zonaras only ascribes to Justin II its renovation and agrees with Cedrenus in attributing the decoration to Tiberius II, Zonaras, *History* 3: 174, 180; *Georgius Cedrenus, Corpus Scriptorum Historiae Byzantinae* 8–9, 2 vols., edited by Immanuel Bekker (Bonn: 1838–1839), vol. 1, 690.

As an octagonal building in the centre of the palace, the Chrysotriklinos opened to many places. The northern vault led to the hall known as the Pantheon and subsequently to the eastern staircase. The Pantheon also opened onto the Phylax, a storehouse for imperial *regalia*. The northeastern vault provided access to the Chapel of St Theodore, where imperial gold and silver objects were kept, along with the Rod of Moses. The eastern vault opened to the Pharos Terrace, while the southeastern vault does not seem to have led anywhere. In contrast, the southern vault led to the private dining room, which in turn provided access to the imperial chambers. From there, it was also possible to pass through to the sea façade or to descend to the Boukoleon Harbour. The southwestern and northwestern vaults lacked doors. Finally, as previously stated, the western one led to the Tripeton after crossing a threshold flanked by two columns.[257] The doors and the cornice were covered with silver during the reign of Constantine VII.[258]

The Chrysotriklinos hosted banquets during Renewal Week and on relevant occasions for the Macedonian dynasty, such as the feast of St Elijah and the anniversary of the consecration of the Nea Ekklesia. The *Kletorologion* of Philotheus explains that the most select guests would be seated at a large central table made of gold that could accommodate thirty people. The remaining guests sat at smaller tables on the sides, each with eighteen places. This brought the total number of guests to 102.[259] However, before being allowed to sit down, a strict protocol was followed. After being introduced into the hall in groups, guests had to prostrate themselves three times before the emperor, then retire and wait on both sides of the great table. Only when all the groups had been introduced were they allowed to sit down.[260] This ritual was similar to that used for receptions, which took place mainly during the promotion of dignitaries. The person being promoted would enter the hall to receive the *insignia*, flanked on either side by members of the court. Once there, he had to perform the three prostrations mentioned above until he reached the emperor's feet, which he had to kiss.[261]

The numerous ceremonies that were held in the hall have provided us with a great deal of information regarding its furnishings. In addition to the curtains, the windows, cornice, and dome were decorated with precious enamels, votive crowns in the colours of the factions and golden doves.[262] The most illustrious

---

[257] *Book of Ceremonies*, 6–7, 22, 79, 96, 108, 114–116, 119, 122–124, 136–137, 147, 162, 169, 171–175, 180, 244, 249, 257–259, 285–292, 300–301, 348, 440, 519, 529, 538–540, 549, 571, 580, 582, 586, 589, 592, 596, 618, 622–625, 633, 640; Oikonomides, *Listes*, 274–275.
[258] *Theophanes Continuatus* 6, 450–451 and 456.   [259] *Book of Ceremonies*, 767–772
[260] *Ibid.*, 70, 86, 89, 90–96, 116, 119, 766–772.
[261] *Ibid.*, 237–248, 257–262, 440–441, 526, 528–530, 622–635, 705–706.
[262] *Ibid.*, 573, 580–582, 586.

object exhibited within the Chrysotriklinos was the Pentapyrgion. It was a cabinet made of gold in the shape of a five-towered building on which precious objects were displayed.[263] At some banquets, the emperor and the patriarch were served at a separate small golden table created by Constantine VII, which was decorated with gems and pearls and placed beneath the eastern vault.[264] A large chandelier was suspended from the centre of the dome.[265] Additionally, the hall was furnished with several couches and thrones. Three of them, made of gold, are attributed to Constantine, Maurice, and Theophilus. A fourth may have belonged to Arcadius (r. 395–408), and there is also a mention of the throne of the Kathisma being brought to the Chrysotriklinos. In addition, two couches were positioned facing each other on either side of the hall: the Couch of Lamentation, where the body of the deceased emperor was displayed, and the Couch of Joy, less documented, but that, following the analogy, might have served to present the newborn heirs before the court. Finally, gold and silver plates were also displayed on a silver stand.[266]

Constantine VII covered the Chrysotriklinos with mosaics depicting a rose garden.[267] However, the main decorative programme dates back to the reign of Michael III (r. 842–867). A poem by Christophorus Mazarinus, a courtier of the mid ninth century, provides a description of the mosaics. The verses mention the emperor and the patriarch, the angelic court, the Virgin, and Christ with a strong triumphant tone proclaiming the extinction of iconoclasm.[268] On the one hand, Christ himself was depicted enthroned just above the imperial throne. Conversely, the Virgin Mary, situated above the western door, acted as an intercessor and a conduit to salvation. In conclusion, by devising this programme, the emperors manifested their subordination to Christ, recognised as the heavenly king and, at the same time, brought an end to more than a century of iconoclastic state policy, validating the veneration of icons in a manner similar to what happened at the Chalke Gate (Figure 29).

---

[263] *Ibid.*, 70, 92, 580, 582, 586, 597, 767. The Pentapyrgion could be moved, and thus was also displayed in the Magnaura on the occasion of imperial wedding rites. See Dagron, '-Architecture d'interieur: le Pentapyrgion', in François Baratte *et al.* (eds.), *Travaux et Mémoires 15: Mélanges Jean-Pierre Sodini* (Paris: ACHCByz, 2005), 109–118; Mabi Angar, 'Furniture and Imperial Ceremony in the Great Palace: Revisiting the Pentapyrgion', in Michael Featherstone *et al.* (eds.), *The Emperor's House: Palaces from Augustus to the Age of Absolutism* (Berlin: De Gruyter, 2015), 181–200.
[264] *Book of Ceremonies*, 70, 92, 95, 520, 771; Oikonomides, *Listes*, 274–275; *Theophanes Continuatus* 6, 450.
[265] *Book of Ceremonies*, 13, 582, 724.
[266] Oikonomides, *Listes*, 274–275; *Book of Ceremonies*, 587.
[267] *Theophanes Continuatus* 6, 456.
[268] *Greek Anthology*, 1, 106. The *Book of Ceremonies*, 7, 22, 94, confirms the presence of Christ in the apse, and other sources place the image of the Virgin above the western door. Zonaras, *History*, vol. 3, 452, 460; Scylitzes, *Synopsis of History*, Leo6, 30.

**Figure 29** Interior of the Chrysotriklinos. Author.

## 4.5 The Pharos Terrace

The Terrace of the Pharos or the Chrysotriklinos extended to the east of the Golden Hall.[269] Further east, the terrace ended in a slope, dominated by the churches of Our Lady of the Pharos, St Elijah, St Demetrius, and several smaller chapels. To the south and west, the terrace was bordered by a gallery known as the *makron* or *stenopos*, which ran from the imperial apartments in the Chrysotriklinos towards the churches.[270] Consequently, the emperor could walk directly across the terrace, in the open air, or through the gallery, under cover, in order to reach the aforementioned churches. The terrace was paved

---

[269] *Book of Ceremonies*, 137, 261, 586.   [270] *Ibid.*, 117, 120.

with marble, and a porphyry *omphalion* marked the position of the emperor (Figure 27).[271]

The Church of the Theotokos of the Pharos was the main chapel of the palace, and housed important relics, including the *arma Christi* (instruments of torture used during the scourging and crucifixion of Christ), the True Cross, the Mandylion, and the Keramion. It also contained a venerable icon of the Virgin, considered to be the Lady of the Palace (*Oikokyra*).[272] The church was constructed by Constantine V (r. 741–775) and was often chosen for imperial weddings.[273] After the Fourth Crusade, the King of France Philip II (r. 1180–1223) acquired the relics, which led to the construction of the Sainte Chapelle in Paris.[274] The church was situated at the southern end of the terrace, in the shadow of the Pharos, after which it was named.[275] It was described by the Patriarch Photius, Nicholas Mesarites, its guardian, and the crusader Robert de Clari.[276] At least after a renovation in the time of Michael III, the church had a narthex with windows and a silver door. The interior was adorned with polychrome marble columns and slabs. A substantial proportion of the ornamentation consisted of silver. The upper walls and vaults were covered with mosaics depicting saints, prophets, and apostles. The central umbrella-shaped dome was surmounted by Christ Pantokrator surrounded by angels, while the apse was crowned by an image of the Virgin of the *orans* type. The iconostasis was constructed using green marble from the sarcophagus of the founder of the church, whose remains were burnt because of his adherence to iconoclasm. The pavement was composed of *sectilia* with zoomorphic motifs and the roof was covered with lead sheets.

The Church of the Pharos was directly connected to the chapel of St Elijah both through the narthex and the interior of the building.[277] This church, built by

---

[271] *Ibid.*, 290; *Vita Basilii*, 90; Anna Comnene, *Alexiad*, 12, 6.

[272] Paul Magdalino, 'L'église du Phare et les reliques de la Passion à Constantinople', in Jannic Durand and Bernard Flusin (eds.), *Byzance et les reliques du Christ* (Paris: Centre De Recherche D'histoire Et Civilisation De Byzance, 2004), 15–30; Michele Bacci, 'La Vergine Oikokyra, signora del Grande Palazzo: Lettura di un passo di Leone Tusco sulle cattive usanze dei greci', *Annali della Scuola Normale Superiore di Pisa: Classe di Lettere e Filosofia* IV, 3, 1 (1998): 261–279.

[273] George the Monk, *Chronicle*, 1065; Symeon, *Chronicle*, 131, 44; *Book of Ceremonies*, 645.

[274] Bernard Flusin, 'Les reliques de la Sainte-Chapelle et leur passé imperial à Constantinople', in Jannic Durand and Marie-Pierre Laffitte (eds.), *Le trésor de la Sainte-Chapelle* (Paris: Réunion des Musées Nationaux, 2001), 20–36.

[275] Nicholas Mesarites, *Coup of John the Fat*, 16.

[276] *The Homilies of Photius, Patriarch of Constantinople*, translation, introduction, and commentary by Cyril Mango (Washington, DC: Dumbarton Oaks Research Library and Collection, 1958), 10, 4–10; Nicholas Mesarites, *Coup of John the Fat*, 12, 16–22; *Robert de Clari. La conquête de Constantinople*, edited by Philippe Lauer (Paris: Librairie Ancienne Edouard Champion, 1974), 82–83.

[277] *Book of Ceremonies*, 116–117.

Basil I, had a circular plan and was surrounded by an annular gallery. The interior was covered with mosaics. It had seven altars, probably corresponding to the same number of niches or apses. The church was used to keep important artefacts such as manuscripts and relics, including those of St Clement and Agathangelus. St Elijah had two chapels attached to it, also constructed by Basil I. One was dedicated to St Clement and the other to Christ the Saviour. The latter was notable for its decoration, comprising gold, gems, pearls, and silver inlay. The railing had silver columns and gold decorations and was presided over by an enamel icon of Christ.[278] It is possible that this chapel might be the same as a rectangular oratory found in the area, paved with a sumptuous *opus sectile* dating from the same period.[279]

The third main church on the terrace was dedicated to St Demetrius by Leo VI (r. 886–912), following a vision in which the saint guaranteed him succession to the throne.[280] The church was described by Gregory, a court official in the mid tenth century.[281] According to his account, the structure was supported by four columns in the shape of a *tetrakion* (monument supported by four columns).[282] The vaults were covered with mosaics depicting a sky full of stars, the walls were adorned with images of saints, and the central dome featured Christ emerging from the sky as the sun. The pavement was inlaid with pearls and enamel. The structure can be considered a canonical example of a cross-in-square Byzantine church, similar to the contemporary foundations of Lips and Myrelaion. Indeed, it is likely to have been one of the earliest examples of this type in Constantinople. The Byzantine infrastructure supporting the Ağası Mahmut Ağa Mosque may be identified with the platform of St Demetrius. Although Bolognesi has identified it with a rather marginal chapel dedicated to St John, it seems more plausible to consider it as Leo's church, given its position and dimensions, which are similar to the aforementioned examples.[283]

Apart from the chapel of St John, St Demetrius was the northernmost church on the terrace, and the position of its main door suggests that it faced the eastern door of the Chrysotriklinos.[284] Moreover, it was also connected with the Church

---

[278] *Vita Basilii*, 87; Nicholas Mesarites, *Coup of John the Fat*, 19, 22.

[279] Marlia M. Mango, 'Polychrome Tiles Found at Istanbul: Typology, Chronology and Function', in Sharon E. J. Gerstel and Julie Lauffenburger (eds.), *A Lost Art Rediscovered: The Architectural Ceramics of Byzantium* (Baltimore: Walters Art Museum-Pennsylvania University Press, 2001), 22–25.

[280] Paul Magdalino, 'Saint Demetrios and Leo VI', *Byzantinoslavica* 51 (1990): 198–201.

[281] Μνημεία αγιολογικά, edited by Theophilos Ioannou (Venice: Τ ύποις Φοίνικος, 1884), 64–65.

[282] The *Book of Ceremonies*, 124 uses the equivalent term *tetraseron*.

[283] Eugenia Bolognesi, 'The End of the Survey of the Boukoleon Harbour and the Beginning of the Survey of the Külliye Kapı Ağası Mahmut Ağa', *Araştırma Sonuçları Toplantıları* 19 (2001): 158–159; the chapel of St John is only mentioned once in *Vita Basilii*, 90.

[284] *Book of Ceremonies*, 124.

## The Great Palace

**Figure 30** Photograph of the Balcony of the Lions by Pierre Tremaux, *ca.* 1850. Wikimedia Commons.

of the Theotokos, likely via the narthex.[285] If this was the case, St Demetrius, St Elijah, and the Theotokos would have been juxtaposed and linked via the narthex, conforming to a layout similar to that observed in the complexes of Lips and Pantokrator.

### 4.6 The Boukoleon

The seaward façade of the palace, known as Boukoleon, extended from the now-lost Belisarius Tower, in Çatladıkapı, to the Pharos tower, spanning over 240 m. Today, it overlooks the Kennedy Cd. The structure comprised two sections. The western one, whose main feature was the Balcony of the Lions (Figure 30), and the eastern one, which corresponded to the loggia known as the House of Justinian (Figure 31). Between them stood the monumental staircase leading to the upper levels.

The Byzantine sources are unanimous in their assertion that the name of the complex originated from a statue of a lion attacking an ox, which was situated in

---
[285] *Ibid.*, 170–171.

**Figure 31** Photograph of the so-called House of Justinian by Guillaume Berggren, *ca*. 1880. Wikimedia Commons.

the harbour, surmounting two columns.[286] The precise date of the monument's construction remains uncertain, but the façade was first referred to by that name in the early ninth century.[287] The monument remained upright at least until the sixteenth century. However, by the late seventeenth century, a description noted that the columns had fallen and the statue had toppled in such a way that it seemed as though the ox was drinking from the sea.[288]

### 4.6.1 The Western Façade

The earliest evidence of this section of the seawalls is found in the Scylitzes manuscript. The illustration depicts with remarkable accuracy the western

---

[286] Anna Comnene, *Alexiad*, 3, 1; Genesius, *On the Reigns of Emperors*, 1, 9; *The History of Leo the Deacon: Byzantine Military Expansion in the Tenth Century*, introduction, translation, and annotation by Alice-Mary Talbot and Denis Sullivan (Washington, DC: Dumbarton Oaks Research Library and Collection, 2005), 5, 7; Scylitzes, *Synopsis of History*, Mich1, 5; Zonaras, *History*, vol. 3, 517.

[287] Cyril Mango, 'The Palace of the Boukoleon', *Cahiers archéologiques, fin de l'Antiquité et Moyen Âge* 45 (1997): 41, n. 2.

[288] Alexander Van Millingen, *Byzantine Constantinople: The Walls of the City and Adjoining Historical Sites* (London: J. Murray, 1899), 270–272.

façade, with the Balcony of the Lions flanking a pavilion, and several poterns on the lower level (fol. 15 r). Despite the relocation of the lions to the Archaeological Museum, the complex was demolished in 1871 to make way for the Orient Express.[289] Nevertheless, numerous travellers from the 18th and 19th centuries made drawings of the monument, providing insight into the appearance of this section of the wall.[290] A number of contributions merit particular attention, including those of Ambroise Tardieu, Thomas Hope, John Foster Junior, Eugène Flandin, and Mary A. Walker. Of special significance is the sole surviving photograph, a daguerreotype taken by Charles Texier in the 1850s (Figure 30). The balcony, which was likely constructed to emphasise a pavilion above, consisted of three blind openings separated by pilasters, resting on what appear to be spoliated triglyphs. The side openings were surmounted by an arch, while the central one was topped by a gable. All three were enclosed by carved marble slabs, resembling doors, similar to those in the upper gallery of Hagia Sophia. The entire composition was guarded by the marble lions standing at either side. Originally, at least the part of the wall to the left of the balcony was flanked by seven arches supported by columns. Two poterns opened at the sea level. To the west of the wall proper, there was another section of brick wall with five broad arches, which extended as far as Çatladıkapı. The whole complex is approximately 150 m long.

The archaeological surveys of the remaining structures at the site revealed that the complex was constructed on multiple layers, with the incorporation of abundant *spolia* from different periods. The earliest dated phases date back to the fifth century.[291] The jetty, built of large blocks of stone, ran along the wall.[292] An inscription on one of the poterns mentions an emperor named Constantine, probably Constantine VII, who is known to have devised the decoration of the palatine harbour with statues of animals.[293]

---

[289] *Ibid.*, 273–274.
[290] Cyril Mango, 'Constantinopolitana', *Jahrbuch des Deutschen Archäologischen Instituts* 80 (1965): 317–323; Cyril Mango, 'Ancient Spolia in the Great Palace of Constantinople', in Doula Mouriki (ed.), *Byzantine East, Latin West: Art Historical Studies in Honor of Kurt Weitzmann* (Princeton: Princeton University Press, 1995), 645–649; Claudia Barsanti, 'Un inedito disegno delle rovine del complesso costantinopolitano del Boukoléon', in Walter Angelelli and Francesca Pomarici (eds.), *Forme e storia: Scritti di arte medievale e moderna per Francesco Gandolfo* (Rome: Artemide, 2011), 45–58; Bardill, 'Visualizing the Great Palace', 28.
[291] Mamboury and Wiegand, *Kaiserpaläste*, 1–3; Bolognesi, *Il Gran Palazzo*, 59–61.
[292] Mamboury and Wiegand, *Kaiserpaläste*, 4–5. [293] Mango, 'Ancient Spolia', 648–649.

### 4.6.2 The Eastern Façade

The so-called House of Justinian extends to the Pharos and is 83 m long. The core of the complex consists of a loggia with seven arches, built with bricks. Marble from older monuments was used for the mouldings, corbels, and balustrades. The balcony was flanked by two pavilions with *tribela* bays (a structure with three openings supported by two columns). Between the eastern pavilion and the Pharos stood an arcade supported by eight white marble columns. In the lower area, another potern was documented, as well as the total thickness of the quay, which reached 12 m.[294] Like the western façade, this section also comprised multiple layers, with the earliest materials dating also to the 5th and 6th centuries.[295] The *tribela* pavilions corresponded to a second phase, with a *terminus post quem* after the seventh century. In contrast, the loggia and the central staircase were added in a third phase, dated from the eighth century onwards.[296] The gallery with the marble columns to the east was dated to the ninth century, and the Pharos was definitely ascribed to the Byzantine period.[297]

### 4.6.3 The Monumental Staircase and the Breakwaters

The monumental staircase situated between the two sections of the wall opened onto the quay through two large arches, 8 m wide and 12 m high. Although the staircase has not been preserved, its infrastructure, consisting of a cistern supported by columns, has survived in fairly good condition.[298] The existence of a primitive staircase or ramp, which would have formed part of a second phase, has been documented as well. In contrast, the present staircase is attributed to a third phase.[299] Furthermore, it is of interest to note that the *Liber Insularum* by Cristophorus Buondelmonti offers insight into the presence of two breakwaters on either side of the complex, which served to protect the Palatine harbour. It seems possible that some vestiges of the western structure may still be extant.[300]

---

[294] Mamboury and Wiegand, *Kaiserpaläste*, 13–17.
[295] *Great Palace: Second Report*, 172–173, 192–193.   [296] *Ibid.*, 189–193.
[297] Eugenia Bolognesi, 'La zona meridionale del Gran Palazzo: Ricognizioni architettoniche e proposte di restauro', in *Il Gran Palazzo*, 59–61.
[298] Mamboury and Wiegand, *Kaiserpaläste*, 9–10, 14.
[299] *Great Palace: Second Report*, 171; Eugenia Bolognesi, 'La zona meridionale del Gran Palazzo', in Eugenia Bolognesi (ed.), *Il Gran Palazzo degli Imperatori di Bisanzio* (Rome: Istituto Italiano di Cultura di Istanbul, 2000), 54–59.
[300] Dominik Heher, 'Der Boukoleonhafen und die angrenzenden Palaststrukturen', *Jahrbuch der Österreichischen Byzantinistik* 64 (2014): 134–135.

### 4.6.4 Chronology of the Sea Wall

Bolognesi and Mango were able to establish a chronology of the successive phases listed above. The earliest infrastructures date back to the fifth century and may be associated with the attribution of the Boukoleon to Theodosius II. The first maritime wall was dated to the sixth century. The second phase is attributed to Justinian II, who is known to have built the first walls of the Lower Palace. The third phase, which encompasses the *tribela* pavilions and the staircase, may have been the work of Theophilus, who extended the terraces overlooking the sea. It is believed that the marble-columned arcade to the east was constructed by Basil I, who also built a bath in the area, while the loggia was probably added by Constantine VII. Finally, many of the entrances were walled during the Late Byzantine period.[301]

### 4.6.5 The Boukoleon in the Sources

As mentioned above, Constantine VII showed a particular interest in enhancing the Boukoleon. He ordered the restoration of the maritime façade and the addition of numerous sculptures. He constructed a fish pond, decorated the imperial apartments above the sea with frescoes, and installed a porphyry fountain topped by a silver eagle in front of them.[302]

In regard to the western façade, it seems reasonable to suggest that the pavilion allegedly situated above the Balcony of the Lions is, in fact, the so-called Porphyra. This chamber was renowned for accommodating the birth of heirs to the throne and other rituals associated with the women of the court. The structure had a square floor plan with a pyramidal roof, and its walls were covered with porphyry. It was the southernmost building of the Lower Palace, and the sole pavilion overlooking the sea, standing above the statue of the lion and the ox.[303] A Venetian witness described the statue of the ox and the lion as standing exactly beneath the Balcony of the Lions.[304] In conclusion, the combination of these accounts situates the Porphyra above the Balcony of the Lions. In this section of the quay, there was also a rarely mentioned monument, namely a fountain or *phiale*, which might be identified with the pool of Constantine VII.

---

[301] Mango, 'Ancient Spolia', 648–649; Eugenia Bolognesi, 'The Monumental Itinerary of the Palatine Harbour of the Boukoleon', *Araştırma Sonuçları Toplantıları* 22 (2004): 54; Bolognesi, 'Gran Palazzo', 237–239.

[302] *Theophanes Continuatus* 6, 447.

[303] Liudprand, *Retribution*, 1, 7; *Theophanes Continuatus* 3, 44; Anna Comnene, *Alexiad*, 6, 8 and 7, 2; Cedrenus, *Synopsis of Histories*, vol. 2, 27; Niketas Choniates, *Annals*, Man1, 5, 168–169.

[304] Van Millingen, *Byzantine Constantinople*, 273–274.

It was positioned there for the guards and imperial sailors, who were always required to be present and ready to serve the emperor.[305]

According to several accounts, the monumental staircase appears to have led directly to the imperial quarters in the Chrysotriklinos.[306] However, a passage must have also extended eastward, through the loggia in the western section, towards the Pharos and the so-called chamber of Nicephorus Phocas, where this emperor was assassinated, as inferred from various sources that mention people accessing the Church of the Theotokos from the harbour.[307] The accounts of several conspiracies related to this chamber deserve further attention. Phocas's executors were hoisted up with ropes from the harbour and led to the chamber where the emperor was sleeping, located directly above the port.[308] Furthermore, the account of an attempted assassination of Alexius Comnenus (r. 1081–1118) provides insight into the fact that this chamber was adjacent to the Theotokos of the Pharos.[309] In particular, it was connected to the southern side of the church.[310] Finally, in connection with this chamber, it is important to mention the Boukoleon staircase, which descended to the polo field and the Nea Ekklesia and should not be confused with the monumental staircase of the harbour. To reach it, the emperors would leave the Chrysotriklinos and walk along the galleries on the southern side of the terrace (the area corresponding to the loggia), until they arrived at the vicinity of the Chamber of Phocas, from where they could descend via the said staircase and reach the Nea.[311]

To conclude, it is worth mentioning the lighthouse. Although the upper portion of the structure has not survived, the Scylitzes Matritensis depicts it topped by four columns (fol. 77 v) (Figure 32). This information is corroborated by the account of a Russian pilgrim, thus reassessing the reliability the miniatures as a source.[312]

---

[305] Dominik Heher and Grigori Simeonov, 'Ceremonies by the Sea: Ships and Ports in Byzantine Imperial Display (4th–12th Centuries)', in Claus Von Carnap-Bornheim (ed.), *Harbours as Objects of Interdisciplinary Research: Archaeology, History and Geosciences* (Mainz: Römisch Germanisches Zentralmuseum-Tagungen, 2018), 227–229.

[306] Anna Comnene, *Alexiad*, 14, 6; William of Tyre, *History of Deeds Done Beyond the Sea*, 20, 23.

[307] Symeon, *Chronicle*, 135, 26, 30; *Theophanes Continuatus* 6, 392–394; Scylitzes, *Synopsis of History*, Const7(1), 10–11; Niketas Choniates, *Annals*, Man1, 4, 130.

[308] Leo the Deacon, *History*, 5, 6–8; Scylitzes, *Synopsis of History*, Niceph2, 22; Zonaras, *History*, vol. 3, 517. See also Niketas Choniates, *Annals*, Man1, 3, 114.

[309] Anna Comnene, *Alexiad*, 12, 6.   [310] Nicholas Mesarites, *Coup of John the Fat*, 17–18.

[311] *Book of Ceremonies*, 117, 120.

[312] George P. Majeska, *Russian Travelers to Constantinople in the Fourteenth and Fifteenth Centuries* (Washington, DC: Dumbarton Oaks Research Library and Collection, 1984), 142.

**Figure 32** The Pharos in the Scylitzes manuscript, second half of the twelfth century. Madrid, BNE, VITR/26/2, fol. 77 v.

## 4.7 Additions to the Lower Palace

### 4.7.1 The First Walls and the Phialai of Justinian II

Concurrent with the construction of his *triklinos*, Justinian II initiated the first expansion of the Lower Palace. Firstly, he constructed a wall surrounding the enclosure, which demonstrates that by the year 700 the Lower Palace was regarded as an integral component of the imperial residence. Subsequently, he devised the *phialai*, ceremonial fountains that were intended to host the receptions of the circus factions, which had previously been held in the Tribunal of Daphne. Despite the common designation of these spaces as 'fountain courts', there is no evidence to suggest that the architectural display extended beyond the basins themselves.[313]

The fountain of the greens was located just below the *triklinos* of Justinian II, dominated by a balcony attached to the hall, which allowed the emperor to observe the performances below. Given its location, it seems highly probable that the basin was located in the garden of the Lausiakos. The *phiale* of the blues stood east of the Pharos Terrace, on a lower level. It was also overlooked by a balustrade at the end of the terrace, in this case surmounted by a baldachin.[314] It is possible that, after the construction of the Triconch, Basil I considered these fountains superfluous and relocated them to the atrium of the Nea Ekklesia.

---

[313] Theoph, AD 6186; Cedrenus, *Synopsis of Histories*, vol. 1, 774; *Patria*, 2, 32.
[314] *Book of Ceremonies*, 284–293, 301–302, 585–586.

### 4.7.2 The Pavilions of Theophilus and Basil I (II)

Theophilus also made considerable contributions to the Lower Palace. Initially, he extended the terraces overlooking the sea and sealed off a cistern, thereby creating space for gardens and pavilions.[315] Subsequently, he directed the construction of a multitude of pavilions situated south of the Chrysotriklinos.

The first pavilion, a three-storey building, was known as Kamilas. The top floor was supported by six green marble columns and the walls were covered with green marble slabs. The interior was adorned with mosaics and paved with white marble. Additionally, the structure comprised two chapels. The imperial library was located on the middle floor. The lower floor was the private dining room, which was directly attached to the Chrysotriklinos. The next pavilion, neighbouring the previous one, was not designated by any specific name. It encompassed two levels. The upper floor was supported by four columns and paved with white marble. The ground floor housed the quarters of the eunuchs in the service of the empress. Later, another hall was built with four rooms supported by mosaic-covered arches, possibly a tetraconch. The floors were made of white marble, and the walls were painted with frescoes. Two of the apses faced northeast towards the second pavilion. The other two, oriented northwestward, were directed towards the Lausiakos. Moreover, this tetraconch was not far from the Porphyra, which, in turn, held the southernmost position on the terrace. The third pavilion, named Mousikos, housed the empress's dressing room. The floor was paved with white marble and the walls decorated with frescoes. Its denomination came from the harmony of the marbles that covered the walls. The edifice was supported by seven white marble columns, five to the south and two to the east. The Mousikos had a twin pavilion attached to the west. Its upper floor was supported by three columns to the south and two to the west. From there a staircase led directly to the empress's chamber in the Chrysotriklinos.[316] Given the functions of this ensemble, it is evident that it was conceived as the *gynaeceum* (women's quarters) of the palace.

Basil I completed Theophilus's expansion with more pavilions and chapels. The most important was the Kainourgion or New Pavilion.[317] However, despite its name, it was in essence a reproduction of Theophilus's Margarites. It consisted of a three-aisled basilica with sixteen columns, eight of green marble and eight of alabaster, carved with vegetal, zoomorphic, and geometric motifs. Attached to the basilica was a square chamber, probably covered by a dome, decorated with mosaics depicting the triumphant emperor and his sons giving thanks to God. The *opus sectile* pavement featured images of peacocks and eagles.[318] The *Book of Ceremonies* provides an accurate description of the

---

[315] *Theophanes Continuatus* 3, 4 and 3, 43.   [316] *Theophanes Continuatus* 3, 43–44.
[317] *Vita Basilii*, 88–90.   [318] *Ibid.*, 89.

location of the Kainourgion. The eastern end of the structure led to the imperial chamber south of the Chrysotriklinos, while the western end gave access to the Tripeton.[319] Not far from here, next to the fourth pavilion of Theophilus, Leo VI erected a chapel in honour of St Anne, whose veneration was particularly appropriate within the women's quarters.[320] To the west of the Kainourgion, Basil I constructed the Pentakouboukleion, a multi-purpose hall where distinguished visitors such as Olga of Kiev were entertained and banquets were held.[321] In addition to this, Basil erected a tetraconch chapel in honour of St Paul, which was subsequently enlarged by his son, Leo, who added a chapel dedicated to St Barbara. The frescoes were later restored by Constantine VII.[322] Further west, outside the palace walls, Basil built a chapel dedicated to St Peter, comprising two smaller oratories dedicated to the Virgin and St Michael.[323]

Lastly, Basil constructed the bath of the Oikonomion on the site of the *phiale* of the blues, situated just behind the apse of the Pharos Church.[324] Consequently, the bath stood in close proximity to the Tzykanisterion, the Nea Ekklesia and the treasury of the church, from which it took its name. The original structure comprised a large pool, seven rooms and twelve porticoes. However, it was largely dismantled by Tzimisces, who spoliated the materials for the construction of the Chalke Church.[325] Despite the extensive plundering, the bath remained in existence until the fourteenth century.[326] As previously mentioned, Bolognesi located these baths in the vicinity of the colonnaded arcade near the Pharos.

### 4.7.3 The Nea Ekklesia and the Tzykanisterion

The Nea Ekklesia, the most significant religious foundation established by Basil I, was situated in close proximity to the palace. It was dedicated to a number of Christian figures, including Christ himself, the Virgin, St Nicholas, St Elijah, and the Archangel Michael. The latter two were the most important patrons, and the emperor regarded them as his personal protectors.[327] The church is primarily described in the biography of its founder, Symeon's chronicle, and in the account of the Arab hostage Harun ibn-Yahya.[328] It had five domes covered in

---

[319] *Book of Ceremonies*, 596, 618.   [320] *Theophanes Continuatus* 3, 43.
[321] *Book of Ceremonies*, 598.   [322] *Theophanes Continuatus* 6, 450.
[323] *Book of Ceremonies*, 122–124, 580.   [324] Nicholas Mesarites, *Coup of John the Fat*, 16.
[325] *Patria*, 1, 60.   [326] Majeska, *Russian Travelers*, 142 and n. 50.
[327] Magdalino, 'Observations on the Nea Ekklesia of Basil I', *Jahrbuch der Österreichischen Byzantinischen* 37 (1987): 51–64.
[328] *Vita Basilii*, 76, 83–86; Harun ibn-Yahya, *Description of Constantinople*, 156–157; Symeon, *Chronicle*, 132, 12–14; *Book of Ceremonies*, 117–120, 571–573, 586, 591; *Patria*, 2, 40; Majeska, *Russian Travelers*, 38 and 96; Giuseppe Gerola, *Le vedute di Costantinopoli di Cristoforo Buondelmonti* (Rome: P. Garroni, 1932), 272.

mosaics. The church could be accessed through ten doors, four of which were crafted from gold and six from silver. Next to the main entrance there was a portrait of the founder and an image of Christ, which may have been ancient sculptures of Solomon and Asclepius, whose identity had been lost over time. The floor was made of *opus sectile* and the walls were covered with polychrome marble. Many of these materials were taken from Justinian's mausoleum in the Holy Apostles. At the time of its foundation, the Nea had an exquisite set of cloths and silks donated by Danielis, Basil's adoptive mother. Its collection of *polykandela* (candelabra) and bronze liturgical objects was also remarkable. Although the church survived until the fall of Byzantium, it was stripped of its exquisite decoration by Isaac Angelos (r. 1185–1195).[329] While the description bears resemblance to churches such as Constantine Lips or St Sophia in Kiev, it is challenging to draw a parallel with the available information.[330] Regardless, there is no doubt that the Nea boasted important dimensions, exquisite decoration, and precious furnishings.

Access to the church was provided by a narthex on the south side of the church, facing the sea, which the emperors used after descending the Boukoleon staircase. Later, they would return to the palace via an elevated passage from a terrace on the roof of the church.[331] The Nea Ekklesia had two courtyards. The western one had two fountains, probably the old *phialai* of the factions. The southern basin was crafted from porphyry with serpents carved around it and had a spout in the form of a pinecone. The fountain was surrounded by columns supporting a cornice with additional spouts. The north basin was constructed from yellow marble and exhibited a comparable display to that of the previous one. Here, the brazen spouts above the cornice had the shape of animals. The eastern courtyard had two arcaded galleries to the north and south, with vaults painted with images of the saints. Between the said porticoes there was a delightful garden. Immediately to the east of this garden lay the Tzykanisterion, next to which stood the church treasury, the aforementioned Oikonomion, and the watchman's house.

The first polo field was built by Theodosius II. Next to it, Michael III built a magnificent stable. Basil I dismantled this Tzykanisterion to allow for the construction of the Nea, and it was subsequently relocated in a slightly more southerly position. The structure was later expanded by Constantine Ducas (r. 1074–1078/1081–1087).[332] A large *triklinos*, the Trikymbalon, was associated

---

[329] Niketas Choniates, *Annals*, Isaac2, 3, 442–443.
[330] Robert Ousterhout, 'Reconstructing Ninth-Century Constantinople', in Leslie Brubaker (ed.), *Byzantium in the Ninth Century: Dead or Alive?* (London: Routledge, 2016), 116–124.
[331] *Book of Ceremonies*, 116–118, 120.
[332] *Patria*, 3, 29; Symeon, *Chronicle*, 131, 27; *Vita Basilii*, 86.

with the polo field. We only know that it was embellished by Basil I with bronze doors taken from the Forum.[333]

Mango, Grotowski, and Effenberger have suggested that the Nea was situated at a considerable distance to the north of the Boukoleon.[334] However, as we have seen, it was attached to the palace, with direct access from the elevated passage and the Boukoleon staircase. Mango's proposed location coincides with a *hagiasma* or sacred spring and the church labelled as San Luca on Vavassore's map of Constantinople. It is highly probable that this is, in fact, the convent of the Hodegetria, renowned for its icon of the Virgin attributed to the Evangelist.[335]

### 4.7.4 The Walls of Nicephorus Phocas

Nicephorus Phocas built a thick wall around the Lower Palace. The wall was composed of two sections. The first commenced at the Tower of Belisarius and the second at the Pharos, both running up north, towards the Upper Palace. The western section ended in a large tower known as the Kentenarion, located at the southern end of the Covered Hippodrome.[336] Some parts of the eastern section survived until the nineteenth century, including a gateway flanked with columns, which has since disappeared.[337]

### 4.7.5 The Comnenian Additions and the Abandonment of the Palace

Manuel Comnenus (r. 1143–1180) added the last pavilions to the Great Palace.[338] The first was called Manouelites after its builder. It was located in the westernmost part of the enclosure, facing the sea. The structure had two floors decorated with porphyry and gold mosaics. Manuel also ordered the porphyry basin from the chamber of Phocas to be moved there. The architectural design of the Manouelites was notably innovative, featuring an audience hall on the first floor, perhaps as a result of Western

---

[333] *Book of Ceremonies*, 586; *Patria*, 3, 206; *Theophanes Continuatus* 6, 438.

[334] Mango, *Brazen House*, 179–182; Piotr Grotowski, 'The Hodegon. Considerations on the Location of the Hodegetria Sanctuary in Constantinople', Δελτίον 27 (2017): 1–61; Arne Effenberger, 'S. Grovus und Aya Yani-Zwei verschwundene Konstantinopeler Kirchen', *Millennium* 17 (2020): 334–343.

[335] Füsun Tülek, 'A Fifth Century Floor Mosaic and a Mural of Virgin of Pege in Constantinople', *Cahiers archéologiques, fin de l'Antiquité et Moyen Âge* 52 (2009): 23–30.

[336] Leo the Deacon, *History*, 4, 6; Niketas Choniates, *Annals*, Andron1, 2, 346; Nicholas Mesarites, *Coup of John the Fat*, 11.

[337] Mamboury and Wiegand, *Kaiserpaläste*, 18–19.

[338] Paul Magdalino, 'Manuel Komnenos and the Great Palace', *Byzantine and Modern Greek Studies* 4 (1978): 101–114.

influence.[339] Thus, the building might have resembled the palaces of Nymphaion and Tekfur Sarayı.[340]

The second pavilion built by Manuel, only known from Mesarites' description, was the Persian-inspired Mouchroutas.[341] The building, attached to the Chrysotriklinos, consisted of two floors connected by a brick staircase decorated with white, green, and blue tiles as well as porphyry slabs. The upper floor was crowned by a dome surrounded by colourfully painted decorations forming recesses. The Islamic influence is evident, evoking the Turkish guests who were welcomed at the Comnenian court, such as John Axouch and the Sultan Kilij Arslan. Indeed, the description of the building makes it almost identical to a pavilion constructed by the latter on the walls of Iconium.[342] The name of the building is a Greek adaptation of the Arabic term 'makhrut', which translates as 'to carve' or 'to sculpt'. This points directly to the presence of *muqarnas*, a decorative system typical of Islamic architecture, and mirrors the roofing of contemporary hybrid Sicilian buildings such as the Capella Palatina in Palermo.[343]

Despite their preference for the Blachernai Palace, situated in the northwestern corner of the city, next to the walls, the Comnenes never abandoned the Great Palace. Indeed, they preferred it as the venue for the most solemn receptions. In any case, the complex was presumably already in a considerable state of decay, with many of its buildings having already stood for several centuries. Isaac II took an unprecedented step, indiscriminately plundering some of the most significant buildings within the palace, including the Chalke Gate and the Nea Ekklesia.[344]

During the reign of his successor, Alexius III (r. 1195–1203), the Great Palace underwent a symbolic demise. The imperial residence was permanently relocated to Blachernae and the races in the Hippodrome were discontinued,

---

[339] Pachymeres, *Relations historiques*, 9, 2; Niketas Choniates, *Annals*, Man1, 3, 114 and 7, 206; Cinnamus, *Deeds of John and Manuel Comnenus*, 4, 14.

[340] Suna Çagaptay, 'How Western Is It? The Palace at Nymphaion and Its Architectural Setting', in Ayla Odekan et al. (eds.), *Change in the Byzantine World in the Twelfth and Thirteenth Centuries* (Istanbul: Vehbi Koç Foundation, 2010), 357–362.

[341] Nicholas Mesarites, *Coup of John the Fat*, 27–28.

[342] Richard P. McClary, *Rum Seljuq Architecture, 1170–1220: The Patronage of Sultans* (Edinburgh: Edinburgh University Press, 2017), 23–38; Lucy-Anne Hunt, 'Comnenian Aristocratic Palace Decoration: Descriptions and Islamic Connections', in Michael Angold (ed.), *The Byzantine Aristocracy: XI to XII Centuries* (Oxford: B.A.R., 1984), 138–156; Asutay-Effenberger, 'Muchrutas: Der seldschukische Schaupavillion im Großen Palast von Konstantinopel', *Byzantion* 74 (2004): 313–324.

[343] Jeremy Johns, 'A Tale of Two Ceilings: The Cappella Palatina in Palermo and the Mouchroutas in Constantinople', in Alison Ohta et al. (eds.), *Art, Trade, and Culture in the Near East and India: From the Fatimids to the Mughals* (London: Gingko Library Art Series, 2016), 56–71.

[344] Niketas Choniates, *Annals*, Isaac2, 3, 442–443.

with Alexius instructing that they be parodied in his new abode.[345] Although the lower part of the palace was still in use during the time of the Latin emperors, these events marked the end of its role as the heart of the Empire, after nearly a thousand years, and foreshadowed the severe institutional and identity crisis that the Byzantines would face after the fall of Constantinople in 1204.

---

[345] *Ibid.*, Alex3, 2, 509.

## THE GREAT PALACE OF CONSTANTINOPLE. ARCHAEOLOGICAL

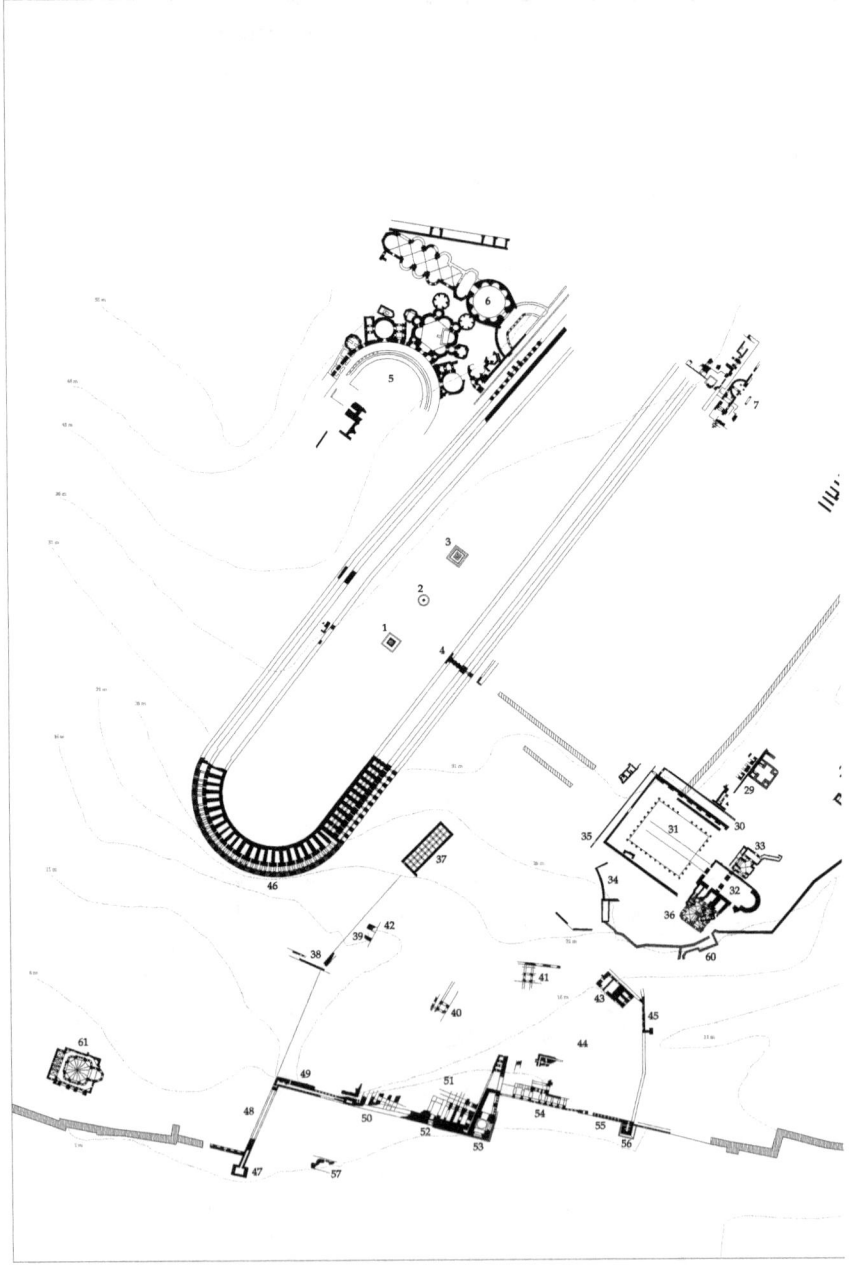

**Plan 1** Archaeological remains of the Great Palace. Also available to view online as supplementary material at www.cambridge.org/calahorra

# The Great Palace

**REMAINS AND ADJOINING SITES**

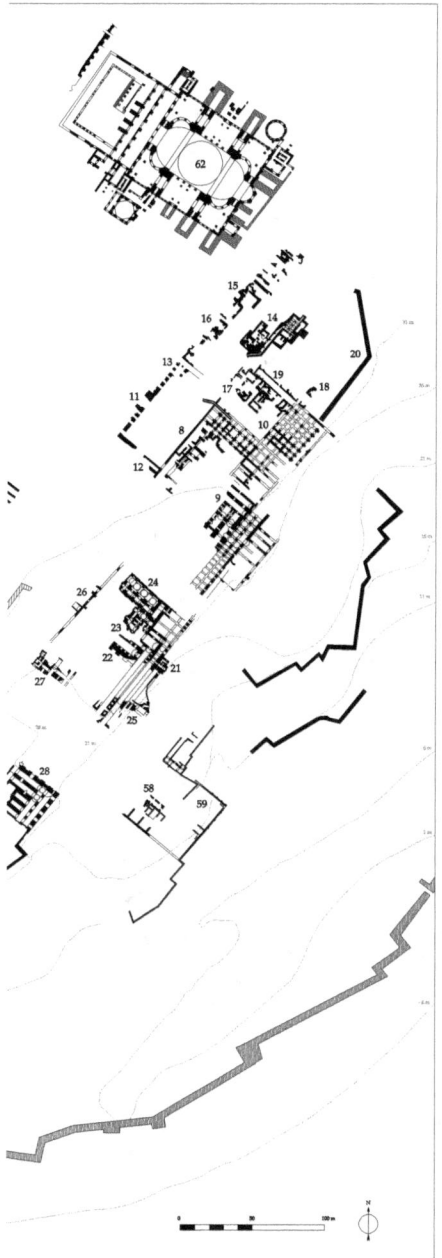

1. Masonry obelisk
2. Delphic tripod
3. Egyptian obelisk
4. H1 pillar
5. Palace of Antiochus
6. So-called Palace of Lausus
7. Baths of Zeuxippos
8. Mamboury Aa
9. Mamboury Ab
10. Mamboury Ac
11. The Chalke Gate
12. Chalke chapel
13. Iron Gate and Chytos
14. Ruins of the Magnaura
15. Remains of an apse
16. Magnaura cistern
17. Justinianic baths
18. Byzantine remains in the Magnaura Terrace
19. Byzantine street separating the Palace and the Magnaura Terrace
20. Magnaura Terrace
21. Mamboury Ba (Ramp House)
22. Mamboury Bb
23. Mamboury Bc, great apse
24. Mamboury Bd
25. Mamboury Be
26. Mamboury Bf
27. Mamboury Bg
28. Mamboury Da
29. Cruciform church
30. Street north of the peristyle
31. Peristyle of the mosaics
32. Apsed hall
33. Mamboury Db
34. G Hall
35. Cubicle
36. Mamboury Dc (Turkish cisterns)
37. Nakilbent cistern
38. Mamboury Fm
39. Mamboury Fl
40. Mamboury Ff
41. Mamboury Fg
42. Byzantine ruins under Hotel Liz
43. Kapı Ağası Mahmut Ağa mosque
44. Chapel paved with sectilia
45. Mamboury Fh (remains of the eastern walls of the Lower Palace)
46. *Sphendone* (curved end) of the Hippodrome
47. Belisarius tower
48. Çatladıkapı
49. Segment of wall with five brick arches
50. Balcony of the lions
51. Boukoleon infrastructures
52. Sea gate
53. Monumental staircase of the Boukoleon
54. House of Justinian
55. Colonnade with eight columns
56. Lighthouse (Pharos)
57. Possible location of the western breakwater
58. *Hagiasma* in Amiral Tafdil Street
59. Mamboury C
60. Byzantine ruins in the vicinity of the Tzykanisterion
61. Church of St. Sergius and Bacchus
62. Hagia Sophia

## THE GREAT PALACE OF CONSTANTINOPLE.

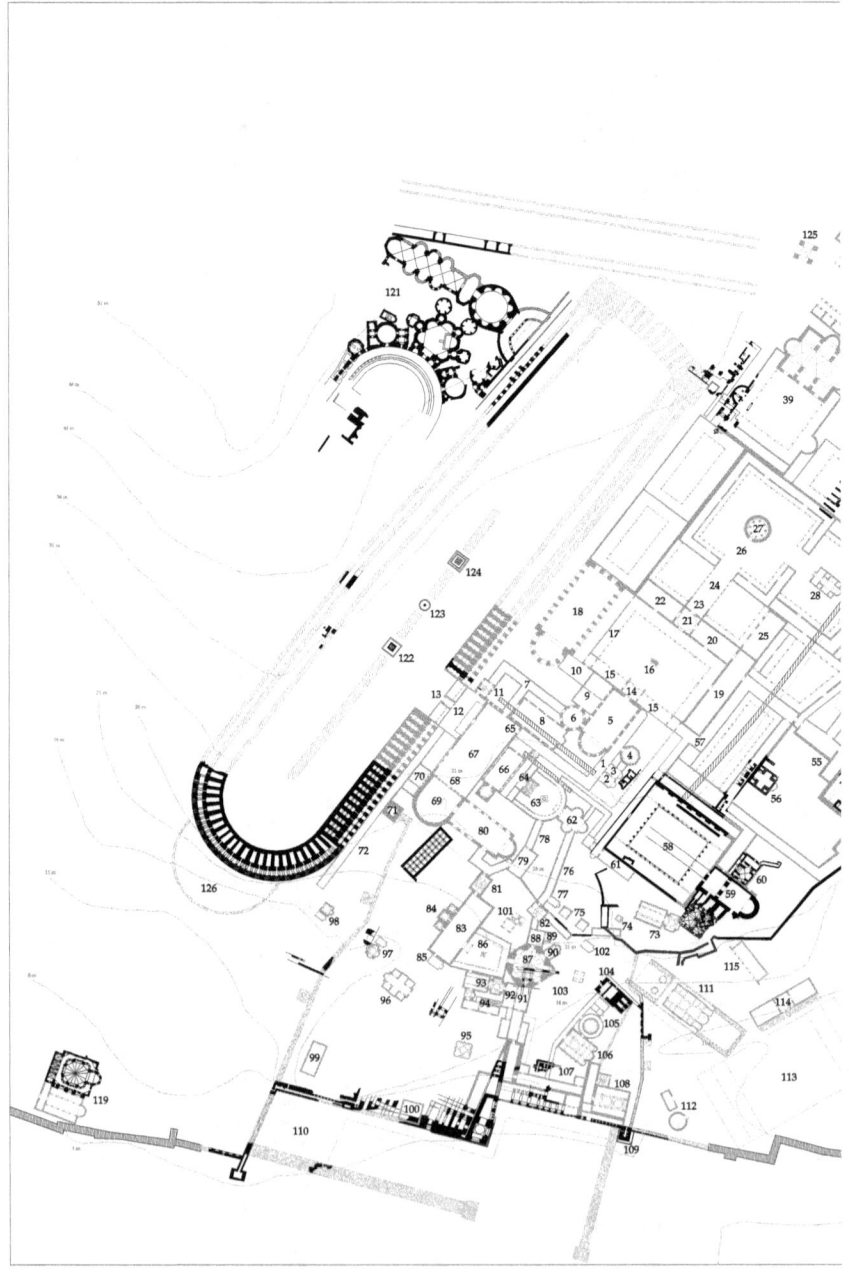

**Plan 2** Integration of the archaeologically documented remains of the Great Palace and our proposed planimetric reconstruction. Also available to view online as supplementary material at www.cambridge.org/calahorra

# The Great Palace

## Hypothetical Plan

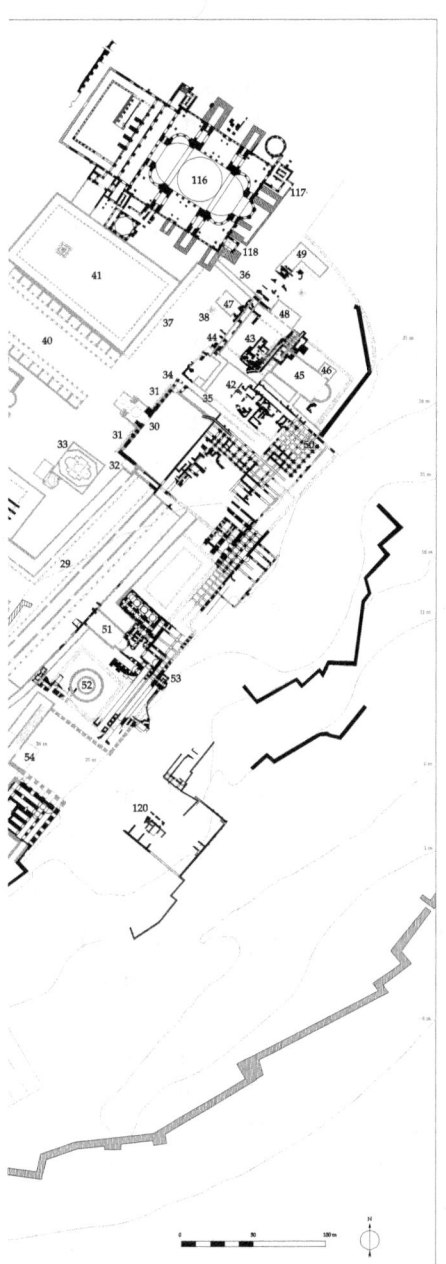

1. Galleries of Daphne
2. Chapel of the Theotokos
3. Chapel of the Trinity
4. Baptistery
5. Augousteus
6. Octagon
7. Galleries of St. Stephen
8. Church of St. Stephen of Daphne
9. Bedchamber of Daphne
10. Office of the *kastresios* (officer in charge of the banquets)
11. *Kochlias* of the Kathisma
12. Kathisma
13. Karea gate
14. *Dikionion*
15. Portico of the Gold Hand
16. Tribunal
17. Portico of the Nineteen Couches
18. *Triklinos* of the Nineteen Couches
19. *Triklinos* of the *kandidatoi*
20. *Triklinos* of the *exkoubitores*
21. The Lamps
22. *Triklinos* of the *scholarioi*
23. Great Gate of the *exkoubitores*
24. The Curtains
25. Stable of the mules
26. First Schola
27. Dome of the Eight Columns or Old Mint
28. Church of the Apostles
29. Porticoes of the Scholai
30. Chalke Gate
31. *Peripatos*
32. Chapel of Christ the Saviour built by Romanus Lecapenus
33. Chapel of Christ the Saviour built by John Tzimisces
34. Iron Gate
35. Chytos
36. *Anabasion*
37. Portico of the Holy Well
38. Column of Eudoxia in the *Pittakia*
39. Baths of Zeuxippos
40. The Regia of the Mese
41. Augoustaion
42. Justinianic baths
43. *Anadendradion* of the Magnaura
44. Augoustaion gate
45. Great *Triklinos* of the Magnaura
46. Bedchamber of the Magnaura
47. Theotokos Varangiotissa or of the Patricians
48. Stables of the augusta
49. Armoury
50. Bridge
51. *Triklinos* of the Ovaton
52. Ovaton
53. Staircase of St. Christina
54. Access by the Church of the Lord
55. Approximate location of the Karianos
56. Church of the Lord
57. Galleries of the Church of the Lord
58. Onopodion
59. Consistorium
60. Small Consistorium
61. Eros
62. Triconch
63. Sigma
64. The Apse, the Pyxites and the Chapel of St. John
65. Iron door of Daphne
66. Thermastra
67. Covered Hippodrome
68. Skyla Gate
69. Skyla
70. *Asekreteia*
71. Kentenarion tower
72. Galleries of Marcian
73. Margarites
74. Aetos and Chapel of the Theotokos
75. Pyramids
76. Galleries of the Fourty Martyrs
77. Chapel of St. Michael Archangel
78. Galleries of the Triconch
79. *Eidikon* storehouse
80. *Triklinos* of Justinian II
81. Western staircase of the Lausiakos
82. Eastern staircase of the Chrysotriklinos, *diaitarikion* and Ivory Gate
83. *Triklinos* Lausiakos
84. Kitchen and garden of the Lausiakos
85. Chapel of St. Basil
86. Horologion / Tripeton
87. Chrysotriklinos
88. Pantheon
89. *Phylax*
90. Chapel of St. Theodore
91. Dining room and Gallery of the Bedchamber
92. Imperial bedchambers
93. Kainourgion
94. Kamilas, pavilion of the eunuchs, Mousikos, anonymous pavilion and Chapel of St. Anne
95. Theophilus' tetraconch
96. Pentakouboukleion
97. Tetraconch of St. Paul and Chapel of St. Barbara
98. Chapel of St. Peter, St. Michael and the Theotokos
99. Manouelites
100. Porphyra
101. Mouchroutas
102. Chapel of St. John
103. Terrace of the Pharos
104. Church of St. Demetrius
105. Church of St. Elijah and Chapels of the Saviour and St. Clement
106. Church of the Theotokos of the Pharos
107. Bedchamber of Phocas
108. Baths of the Oikonomaion and Boukoleon staircase
109. Pharos
110. Boukoleon Harbour
111. Nea Ekklesia
112. Oikonomaion
113. Tzykanisterion
114. Trikymbalon *triklinos*
115. Stables
116. Hagia Sophia
117. Chapel of St. Nicholas
118. Chapel of the Holy Well
119. Churches of St. Sergius and Bacchus and St. Peter and Paul
120. Approximate location of the Theotokos Hodegetria
121. Palaces of Antiochus and Lausus
122. Masonry obelisk
123. Delphic Tripod
124. Egyptian obelisk
125. Million
126. Hippodrome of St. Sergius

# Bibliography

## Sources

*Accounts of Medieval Constantinople: The Patria*, translated by Albrecht Berger (Washington, DC: Dumbarton Oaks Research Library and Collection, 2013).

*Acta Conciliorum Oecumenicorum. Series secunda. Concilium Universale Constantinopolitanum Tertium*, edited by Rudolf Riedinger (Berlin: De Gruyter, 1990–1992).

*Chronicon Paschale 284–628*, translated with introduction and notes by Mary Whitby and Michael Whitby (Liverpool: Liverpool University Press, 1989).

*Chronographiae quae Theophanis Continuati nomine fertur Liber quo Vita Basilii Imperatoris amplectitur, Corpus Fontium Historiae Byzantinae* 42, edited and translated by Ihor Ševčenko (Berlin: De Gruyter, 2011).

*Chronographiae quae Theophanis Continuati nomine fertur Libri I–IV, Corpus Fontium Historiae Byzantinae* 53, edited and translated by Michael Featherstone and Juan Signes Codoñer (Berlin: De Gruyter 2015).

*Constantin VII Porphyrogénète. Le Livre des Cérémonies, Corpus Fontium Historiae Byzantinae* 52, 6 vols., edited and translated by Gilbert Dagron and Bernard Flusin (Paris: Association des amis du Centre d'Histoire et Civilisation de Byzance, 2020).

*Constantine Porphyrogennetos: The Book of Ceremonies*, 2 vols., translated by Ann Moffat and Maxeme Tall (Canberra: Australian Association for Byzantine Studies, 2012).

*Corpus iuris civilis*, 3 vols., edited by Theodor Mommsen, Paul Krueger, Rudolf Schoell, and Wilhelm Kroll (Berlin: Weidmann, 1888–1895).

*Eusebius: Life of Constantine*, introduction, translation, and commentary by Averil Cameron and Stuart G. Hall (Oxford: Clarendon Press, 1999).

*Georges Pachymérès. Relations historiques, Corpus Fontium Historiae Byzantinae* 24, 5 vols., edited and translated by Albert Failler and Vitalien Laurent (Paris: Les Belles Lettres, 1984–2000).

*Georgius Cedrenus, Corpus Scriptorum Historiae Byzantinae* 8–9, 2 vols., edited by Immanuel Bekker (Bonn, 1838–1839).

*Georgius Monachus, Patrologiae Cursus Completus, Series Graeca* 110, edited by Jean Paul Migne (Paris, 1863).

*In Laudem Iustini Augusti Minoris Libri IV*, translated by Averil Cameron (Bristol: The Athlone Press, 1976).

*Ioannes Lydus: On Powers or the Magistracies of the Roman State*, translated and edited by Anastasius C. Bandy (Philadelphia: American Philosophical Society, 1983).

*Ioannis Cantacuzeni Eximperatoris Historiarum Libri IV, Corpus Scriptorum Historiae Byzantinae* 5–7, 3 vols., edited by Ludwig Schopen (Bonn, 1828–1832).

*Ioannis Zonarae Epitomae historiarum, Corpus Scriptorum Historiae Byzantinae* 47–49, 3 vols., edited by Moritz E. Pinder and Theodor Büttner-Wobst (Bonn, 1897).

*John Kinnamos*: *Deeds of John and Manuel Comnenus*, translated by Charles M. Brand (New York: Columbia University Press, 1976).

*John of Ephesus: Lifes of the Eastern Saints* (II), *Patrologia Orientalis* 18, Syriac text edited and translated by Edmund W. Brooks (Paris: Firmin Didot, 1924).

*John Scylitzes: A Synopsis of Byzantine History, 811–1057*, translated with introduction, text, and notes by John Wortley (Cambridge: Cambridge University Press, 2010).

*Joseph Genesius: On the Reigns of the Emperors*, translation and commentary by Anthony Kaldellis (Canberra: Australian Association for Byzantine Studies, 1998).

*Les listes de préséance byzantines des IXe et Xe siècles*, introduction, text, translation, and commentary by Nikolaos Oikonomides (Paris: CNRS, 1972).

*Nicholas Mesarites: His Life and Works in Translation*, translated with notes and commentary by Michael Angold (Liverpool: Liverpool University Press, 2017).

*O City of Byzantium: Annals of Niketas Choniates*, translated by Harry J. Magoulias (Detroit: Wayne State University Press, 1984).

*Procopius, with an English Translation*, 6 vols., translated by Henry B. Dewing (London: William Heinemann, 1914–1940).

*Robert de Clari. La conquête de Constantinople*, edited by Philippe Lauer (Paris: Librairie Ancienne Edouard Champion, 1974).

*Socrate de Constantinople. Histoire ecclésiastique*, 4 vols., introduction, notes, and translation by Paul Maraval and Pierre Périchon (Paris: Éditions du Cerf, 2004–2007).

*Sozomène. Histoire ecclésiastique*, 4 vols., introduction, notes, and translation by André-Jean Festugière, Bernard Grillet, and Guy Sabbah (Paris: Éditions du Cerf, 1983).

*Symeonis Magistri Annales, Corpus Scriptorum Historiae Byzantinae* 45, edited by Immanuel Bekker (Bonn, 1838).

*The Alexiad*, translated by Peter Frankopan and Edgar R. A. Sewter (London: Penguin, 2009).

*The Chronicle of John Malalas*, translated by Elizabeth Jeffreys, Michael Jeffreys, and Roger Scott (Canberra: Australian Association for Byzantine Studies, 1986).

*The Chronicle of Marcellinus*, with a translation and commentary by Brian Croke (Sydney: Australian Association for Byzantine Studies, 1995).

*The Chronicle of the Logothete*, translated with introduction, commentary, and indices by Staffan Wahlgren (Liverpool: Liverpool University Press, 2019).

*The Chronicle of Theophanes Confessor: Byzantine and Near Eastern History, AD 284–813*, translated with introduction and commentary by Cyril Mango and Roger Scott (Oxford: Clarendon Press, 1997).

*The Complete Works of Liudprand of Cremona*, translated by Paolo Squatriti (Washington, DC: Catholic University of America Press, 2007).

*The Greek Anthology, with an English Translation*, 5 vols., translated by William R. Patton (London: W. Heinemann, 1916–1918).

*The History of Leo the Deacon: Byzantine Military Expansion in the Tenth Century*, introduction, translation, and annotation by Alice-Mary Talbot and Denis Sullivan (Washington, DC: Dumbarton Oaks Research Library and Collection, 2005).

*The History of Theophylact Simocatta*, translated by Mary Whitby and Michael Whitby (Oxford: Clarendon Press, 1986).

*The Homilies of Photius, Patriarch of Constantinople*, translation, introduction, and commentary by Cyril Mango (Washington, DC: Dumbarton Oaks Research Library and Collection, 1958).

*The Notitia Urbis Constantinopolitanae*, translated by John Matthews, in Lucy Grig and Galvin Kelly (eds.), *Two Romes: Rome and Constantinople in Late Antiquity* (Oxford: Oxford University Press, 2012), 81–115.

*The Novels of Justinian*, translated and annotated by David J. D. Miller and Peter Sarris (Cambridge: Cambridge University Press, 2018).

*The Rise and Fall of Nikephoros II Phokas*, notes and translation by Denis Sullivan (Leiden: Brill, 2018).

Vasiliev, Alexander, 'Harun ibn-Yahya and his description of Constantinople', *Seminarium Kondakovianum* 5 (1932): 149–163.

*William of Tyre: A History of Deeds Done Beyond the Sea*, 2 vols., translated and annotated by Emily A. Babcock and August C. Krey (New York: Columbia University Press, 1943).

Zosime. *Histoire nouvelle*, 3 vols., edited and translated by François Paschoud (Paris: Les Belles Lettres, 1971–1989).

Μνημεία αγιολογικά, edited by Theophilos Ioannou (Venice: Τύποις Φοίνικος, 1884).

## Literature

Akyürek, Engin, *The Hippodrome of Constantinople* (Cambridge: Cambridge University Press, 2021).

Angar, Mabi, 'Furniture and Imperial Ceremony in the Great Palace: Revisiting the Pentapyrgion', in Michael Featherstone, Jean-Michel Spieser, Gülru Tanman, and Ulrike Wulf-Rheidt (eds.), *The Emperor's House: Palaces from Augustus to the Age of Absolutism* (Berlin: De Gruyter, 2015), 181–200.

Artan, Tülay, 'The Making of the Sublime Porte Near the Alay Köskü and a Tour of a Grand Vizierial Palace at Sülemaniye', *Turcica* 43 (2011): 145–206.

Asutay-Effenberger, Neslihan, 'Muchrutas: Der seldschukische Schaupavillion im Großen Palast von Konstantinopel', *Byzantion* 74 (2004): 313–324.

Asutay-Effenberger, Neslihan and Arne Effenberger, 'Zur Kirche auf einem Kupferstich von Gugas İnciciyan und zum Standort der Chalke-Kirche', *Byzantinische Zeitschrift* 97, 1 (2008): 51–94.

Athanasiou, Fani, Benetia Malama, and Maria Miza, 'Η Βασιλική του Γαλεριανού Συγκροτήματος', *Αρχαιολογικό Έργο στη Μακεδονία και Θράκη* 12 (1998): 113–126.

Auzépy, Marie-France, 'La destruction de l'icône du Christ par Léon III: Propagande ou realité?', *Byzantion* 60 (1990): 445–492.

Bacci, Michele, 'La Vergine Oikokyra, signora del Grande Palazzo: Lettura di un passo di Leone Tusco sulle cattive usanze dei greci', *Annali della Scuola Normale Superiore di Pisa: Classe di Lettere e Filosofia* IV, 3, 1 (1998): 261–279.

Baldini-Lippolis, Isabella, 'Lo skeuophylakion nell'architettura protobizantina', in Isabella Baldini-Lippolis and Anna L. Morelli (eds.), *Oro sacro: Aspetti religiosi ed economici da Atene a Bisanzio* (Bologna: Ante Quem, 2014), 123–138.

Baldini-Lippolis, Isabella and Salvatore Cosentino, 'Rituali di corte: Il Triclinio dei XIX Letti del Grande Palazzo di Costantinopoli', *Byzantinische Zeitschrift* 114, 1 (2021): 65–110.

Bardill, Jonathan, *Brickstamps of Constantinople*, 2 vols. (Oxford: Oxford University Press, 2004).

Bardill, Jonathan, 'The Great Palace and the Walker Trust Excavations', *Journal of Roman Archaeology* 12 (1999): 217–230.

Bardill, Jonathan, 'Visualizing the Great Palace of the Byzantine Emperors at Constantinople: Archaeology, Text, and Topography', in Franz A. Bauer (ed.), *Visualisierungen von Herrschaft: Frühmittelalterliche Residenzen – Gestalt und Zeremoniell; Internationales Kolloquium 3./4. Juni 2004 in Istanbul* (Istanbul: Ege Yayınlar, 2006), 5–46.

Barsanti, Claudia, 'Un inedito disegno delle rovine del complesso costantinopolitano del Boukoléon', in Walter Angelelli and Francesca Pomarici (eds.), *Forme e storia: Scritti di arte medievale e moderna per Francesco Gandolfo* (Rome: Artemide, 2011), 45–58.

Berger, Albrecht, 'The Byzantine Court as Physical Space', in Ayla Ödekan, Nevra Necipoğlu, and Engin Akyürek (eds.), *The Byzantine Court: Source of Power and Culture; Papers from the Second International Sevgi Gönül Byzantine Studies Symposium* (Istanbul: Koç University Press, 2010), 12–22.

Berger, Albrecht, 'Die Senate von Konstantinopel', *Boreas* 18 (1995): 131–142.

Berger, Albrecht and Jonathan Bardill, 'The Representations of Constantinople in Hartmann Schedel's World Chronicle, and Related Pictures', *Byzantine and Modern Greek Studies* 22 (1998): 1–37.

Biasci, Andrea, A., 'Il padiglione del "Tempio di Minerva Medica" a Roma: Struttura, tecniche di costruzione e particolari inediti', *Science and Technology for Cultural Heritage* 9 (2000): 1–22.

Bolognesi, Eugenia, 'The End of the Survey of the Boukoleon Harbour and the Beginning of the Survey of the Külliye Kapı Ağası Mahmut Ağa', *Araştırma Sonuçları Toplantıları* 19 (2001): 158–159.

Bolognesi, Eugenia, 'The Great Palace of Constantinople: An Introduction to the Main Areas of Activity, Ground Levels and Phases of Development', in Werner Jobst, Raimund Kastler, and Veronika Scheibelreiter (eds.), *Neue Forschungen und Restaurierungen im Byzantinischen Kaiserpalast von Istanbul: Akten der Internationalen Fachtagung vom 6.-8. November 1991* (Vienna: Österreichische Akademie der Wissenschaften, 1999), 9–16.

Bolognesi, Eugenia, 'The Great Palace Itineraries', *Araştırma Sonuçları Toplantıları* 26 (2006): 197–210.

Bolognesi, Eugenia, 'Il Gran Palazzo', *Bizantinistica* 2 (2000): 197–242.

Bolognesi, Eugenia, 'La zona meridionale del Gran Palazzo: Ricognizioni architettoniche e proposte di restauro', in Eugenia Bolognesi (ed.), *Il Gran Palazzo degli Imperatori di Bisanzio* (Rome: Istituto Italiano di Cultura di Istanbul, 2000), 59–61.

Bolognesi, Eugenia, 'The Monumental Itinerary of the Palatine Harbour of the Boukoleon', *Araştırma Sonuçları Toplantıları* 22 (2004): 53–62.

Bolognesi, Eugenia, 'The Scholae of the Master of the Offices as the Palace Praetorium', *Anatolia Antiqua* 16 (2008): 231–257.

Brett, Gerard, Günter Martiny, and Robert B. K. Stevenson, *The Great Palace of the Byzantine Emperors: Being a First Report on the Excavations Carried Out in Istanbul on Behalf of the Walker Trust (The University of St. Andrews) 1935–1938* (Oxford: Oxford University Press, 1947).

Brubaker, Leslie, *Inventing Byzantine Iconoclasm* (London: Bristol Classical Press, 2012).

Brubaker, Leslie and John Haldon, *Byzantium in the Iconoclast Era, c. 680–850: A History* (Cambridge: Cambridge University Press, 2011).

Çagaptay, Suna, 'How Western Is It? The Palace at Nymphaion and Its Architectural Setting', in Ayla Ödekan, Engin Akyürek, and Nevra Necipoğlu (eds.), *Change in the Byzantine World in the Twelfth and Thirteenth Centuries* (Istanbul: Vehbi Koç Foundation, 2010), 357–362.

Calahorra, Alfredo, 'El marfil de Tréveris una iconografía clave en el contexto de la propaganda político-religiosa del Triunfo de la Ortodoxia', *Erytheia* 39 (2018): 9–53.

Calahorra, Alfredo, 'On the toponymics of the Great Palace of Constantinople: The Daphne', *Byzantinische Zeitschrift* 115 (2022): 1–29.

Cameron, Averil, *Procopius and the Sixth Century* (London: Routledge, 1985).

Carandini, Andrea, Andreina Ricci, and Mariette de Vos, *Filosofiana: La Villa de Piazza Armerina* (Palermo: Atlante, 1982).

Carlier, Patricia, 'Recherches archaeologiques au Château de Qastal (Jordanie)', *Annual of the Department of Antiquities of Jordan* 28 (1984): 343–383.

Ćurčić, Slobodan, 'Late-Antique Palaces: The Meaning of Urban Context', *Ars Orientalis* 33 (1993): 67–90.

Cutler, Anthony, 'Barberiniana: Notes on the Making, Content, and Provenance of Louvre OA. 9063', in Anthony Cutler, *Late Antique and Byzantine Ivory Carving* (Aldershot: Ashgate Variorum, 1998), 329–339.

Cutler, Anthony, 'The Elephants of the Great Palace Mosaic', *Bulletin d'information de l'Association internationale pour l'étude de la mosaïque antique* 10 (1985): 125–131.

Dagron, Gilbert, 'Architecture d'interieur: Le Pentapyrgion', in Baratte, François, Vincent Déroche, Catherine Jolivet-Lévy, and Brigitte Pitarakis (eds.), *Travaux et Mémoires 15. Mélanges Jean-Pierre Sodini* (Paris: ACHCByz, 2005), 109–118.

Dark, Ken, 'Roman Architecture in the Great Palace of the Byzantine Emperors at Constantinople during the Sixth to Ninth Centuries', *Byzantion* 77 (2007): 87–105.

de Capitani D'Arzago, Alberto, *Il Circo Romano: Ricerche della Commissione per la forma urbis Mediolani* (Milan: Ceschina, 1939).

Delmaire, Roland, *Les institutions du Bas-Empire romain, de Constantin à Justinien I: Les institutions civiles palatines* (Paris: Éditions du Cerf and Éditions du CNRS, 1995).

Denker, Asuman, 'Excavations at the Great Palace', in Ayla Ödekan, Nevra Necipoğlu, and Engin Akyürek (eds.), *The Byzantine Court: Source of Power and Culture; Papers from the Second International Sevgi Gönül Byzantine Studies Symposium* (Istanbul: Koç University Press, 2010), 13–18.

Denker, Asuman, Gülcay Yagzi, and Ayşe B. Akay, 'Former Sultanahmet Prison', in Selmin Kangal (ed.), *Istanbul: 8000 Years Brought to Daylight: Marmaray, Metro, Sultanahmet Excavations* (Istanbul: Koç University Press, 2007), 126–141.

Dunbabin, Katherine, 'The Triumph of Dionysus on Mosaics in North Africa', *Papers of the British School at Rome* 39 (1979): 52–65.

Ebersolt, Jean, *Le Grand Palais de Constantinople et le Livre des Cérémonies* (Paris: Ernest Leroux, 1910).

Effenberger, Arne, 'S. Grovus und Aya Yani-Zwei verschwundene Konstantinopeler Kirchen', *Millennium* 17 (2020): 334–343.

Eyice, S., 'Arslanhane ve Çevresinin Arkeolojisi', *İstanbul Arkeoloji Müzeleri Yıllığı* 11–12 (1964): 23–33.

Featherstone, Michael, 'The Chrysotriklinos as Seen Through De Cerimoniis', in Lars M. Hoffmann and Anuscha Monchizadeh (eds.), *Zwischen Polis, Provinz und Peripherie: Beiträge zur byzantinischen Geschichte und Kultur* (Weisbaden: Harrassowitz Verlag, 2005), 833–840.

Featherstone, Michael, 'The Everyday Palace in the Tenth Century', in Michael Featherstone, Jean-Michel Spieser, Gülru Tanman, and Ulrike Wulf-Rheidt (eds.), *The Emperor's House. Palaces from Augustus to the Age of Absolutism* (Berlin: De Gruyter, 2015), 149–158.

Featherstone, Michael, 'Theophilus's Margarites: The 'Apsed Hall' of the Walker Trust?' in Silvia Pedone and Andrea Paribeni (eds.), *«Di Bisanzio dirai ciò che è passato, ciò che passa e che sarà» Scritti in onore di Alessandra Guiglia* (Rome: Bardi Edizioni, 2018), 173–186.

Flusin, Bernard, 'Les reliques de la Sainte-Chapelle et leur passé imperial à Constantinople', in Jannic Durand and Marie-Pierre Laffitte (eds.), *Le trésor de la Sainte-Chapelle* (Paris: Réunion des Musées Nationaux, 2001), 20–36.

Gerola, Giuseppe, *Le vedute di Costantinopoli di Cristoforo Buondelmonti* (Rome: P. Garroni, 1932).

Girgin, Çiğdem, 'La porte monumentale trouvée dans les fouilles près de l'ancienne prison de Sultanahmet', *Anatolia Antiqua* 16 (2008): 259–290.

Golvin, Jean-Claude and Fabricia Fauquet, 'L'hippodrome de Constantinople: Essais de restitution architecturale du dernier état du monument', *Antiquité Tardive* 15 (2007): 181–214.

Grotowski, Piotr, 'The Hodegon: Considerations on the Location of the Hodegetria Sanctuary in Constantinople', *Δελτίον* 27 (2017): 1–61.

Guilland, Rodolphe, *Études de topographie de Constantinople byzantine*, 2 vols. (Berlin: Adolf Hakkert, 1969).

Habas, Lihi, 'Camel Caravans and Trade in Exotic Animals in the Mosaics of the Desert Margin', in Leah di Segni (ed.), *Man Near a Roman Arch: Studies Presented to Prof. Yoram Tsafrir* (Jerusalem: Israel Exploration Society, 2009), 54–73.

Hayes, John W., *Late Roman Pottery: A Catalogue of Roman Fine Wares* (London: The British School at Rome, 1972).

Heher, Dominik, 'Der Boukoleonhafen und die angrenzenden Palaststrukturen', *Jahrbuch der Österreichischen Byzantinistik* 64 (2014): 119–137.

Heher, Dominik and Grigori Simeonov, 'Ceremonies by the Sea: Ships and Ports in Byzantine Imperial Display (4th–12th Centuries)', in Claus Von Carnap-Bornheim (ed.), *Harbours as Objects of Interdisciplinary Research: Archaeology, History and Geosciences* (Mainz: Römisch Germanisches Zentralmuseum-Tagungen, 2018), 221–248.

Hellenkemper-Salies, Gisela, 'Die Datierung der Mosaiken im Großen Palast zu Konstantinopel', in Jean Pierre Darmon and Alain Rebourg (eds.), *La mosaïque gréco-romaine 4: IVe Colloque international pour l'étude de la mosaïque antique*, Trèves 8–14 août 1984 (Paris: Association internationale pour l'étude de la mosaïque antique, 1994), 273–308.

Humphrey, John H., *Roman Circuses: Arenas for Chariot Racing* (London: Batsford, 1986).

Hunt, Lucy-Anne, 'Comnenian Aristocratic Palace Decoration: Descriptions and Islamic Connections', in Michael Angold (ed.), *The Byzantine Aristocracy: XI to XII Centuries* (Oxford: B.A.R., 1984), 138–156.

Janin, Raymond, *La géographie ecclésiastique de l'Empire Byzantin, Le siège de Constantinople et le patriarcat oecuménique, vol. 3: Les églises et les monastères* (Paris: Institut Français d'Études Byzantines, 1969).

Jobst, Werner, 'Archäologie und Denkmalpflege im Bereich des Großen Palastes von Konstantinopel', *Araştırma Sonuçları Toplantıları* 11 (1993): 9–18.

Jobst, Werner, *Mosaikenforschung im Kaiserpaläste von Konstantinopel* (Vienna: Verlag der Österreichischen Akademie der Wissenschaften, 1992).

Jobst, Werner, Behçet Erdal, and Christian Gurtner, *Istanbul: The Great Palace Mosaic* (Istanbul: Arkeoloji ve Sanat Yayınları, 1997).

Johns, Jeremy, 'A Tale of Two Ceilings: The Cappella Palatina in Palermo and the Mouchroutas in Constantinople', in Alison Ohta, Michael Rogers, and Rosalind W. Haddon (eds.), *Art, Trade, and Culture in the Near East and India: From the Fatimids to the Mughals* (London: Gingko Library Art Series, 2016), 56–71.

Johnson, Mark J., *Roman Imperial Mausoleum in Late Antiquity* (Cambridge: Cambridge University Press, 2014).

Johnson, Mark J., 'Towards a History of Theoderic's Building Programme', *Dumbarton Oaks Papers 42* (1988): 73–96.

Karamberi, Marianna, 'Ο ρολός του Οκταγώνου στο Γαλεριανού συγκρότημα και η σχέση του με το μεγάλο περιστύλιο', *Αρχαιολογικά Ανάλεκτα εξ Αθηνών* 23–28 (1990–1996): 116–128.

Kostenec, Jan, 'Chrysotriklinos', in *Encyclopaedia of the Hellenic World* [http://constantinople.ehw.gr/forms/fLemmaBodyExtended.aspx?lemmaID=12440, retrieved 3 January 2021].

Kostenec, Jan, 'The Heart of the Empire: The Great Palace of the Byzantine Emperors Reconsidered', in Ken Dark (ed.), *Secular Buildings and the Archaeology of Everyday Life in the Byzantine Empire* (Oxbow: Oxbow Books, 2004), 4–36.

Kostenec, Jan, 'Observations on the Great Palace at Constantinople: The Sanctuaries of the Archangel Michael, the Daphne Palace, and the Magnaura', *Reading Medieval Studies* 31 (2005): 27–35.

Krautheimer, Richard, 'Die Dekaenncakkubita in Konstantinopel: Ein kleiner Beitrag zur Frage Rom und Byzanz', in Richard Krautheimer, *Ausgewählte Aufsätze zur europäischen Kunstgeschichte* (Cologne: Dumont, 1988), 195–199.

Labarte, Jules, *Le Palais impérial de Constantinople et ses abords, Sainte Sophie, le Forum Augustéon et l'Hippodrome, tels qu'ils existaient au Xe siècle* (Paris: Victor Didron, 1861).

Lavan, Luke, 'Late Antique Governors' Palaces: A Gazetteer', *Antiquité Tardive* 7 (2000): 135–164.

Lazarev, Victor I., 'Фрески Кастельсеприо (К критике теории Вейцмана о «Македонском Ренессансе»)', *Византийский Временник* 7 (1953): 359–378.

Lemerle, Paul, *Le premier humanisme byzantin: Notes et remarques sur enseignement et culture à Byzance, des origines au Xe siècle* (Paris: Presses Universitaires de France, 1971).

Levi, Doro, *Antioch Mosaic Pavements* (Princeton: Princeton University Press, 1947).

*Lexicon Iconographicum Mythologiae Classicae*, vol. 3 (Zurich-Munich: Artemis Verlag, 1986).

Luchterhandt, Martin, 'Päpstlicher Palastbau und höfisches Zeremoniell unter Leo III.', in Christoph Stiegemann and Matthias Wemhoff (eds.), *799. Kunst und Kultur der Karolingerzeit: Karl der Große und Leo III.* (Mainz: Philipp von Zabern, 1999), 109–122.

Macchiarella, Gianclaudio, 'Date and Patron(s) of the Floor Mosaic of the Great Palace of the Emperors: A New Approach', in Gianclaudio Macchiarella (ed.), *Alpaghian: Raccolta di scritti in onore di Adriano Alpago Novello* (Naples: ScriptWeb, 2005).

MacCormack, Sabine G., *Art and Ceremony in Late Antiquity* (Berkeley: University of California Press, 1981).

Magdalino, Paul, 'L'église du Phare et les reliques de la Passion à Constantinople', in Jannic Durand and Bernard Flusin (eds.), *Byzance et les reliques du Christ* (Paris: Centre de Recherche d'histoire et Civilisation de Byzance, 2004), 15–30.

Magdalino, Paul, 'Manuel Komnenos and the Great Palace', *Byzantine and Modern Greek Studies* 4 (1978): 101–114.

Magdalino, Paul, 'Modes of Reconstruction in Byzantine Constantinople', in Emmanuelle Capet, Cécile Dogniez, Maria Gorea, Renée Koch Piettre, Francesco Massa, and Hedwige Rouillard-Bonraisin (eds.), *Reconstruire les villes: Modes, motifs et récits* (Turnhout: Brepols, 2019), 255–267.

Magdalino, Paul, 'Observations on the Nea Ekklesia of Basil I', *Jahrbuch der Österreichischen Byzantinischen* 37 (1987): 51–64.

Magdalino, Paul, 'Saint Demetrios and Leo VI', *Byzantinoslavica* 51 (1990): 198–201.

Majeska, George P., *Russian Travelers to Constantinople in the Fourteenth and Fifteenth Centuries* (Washington, DC: Dumbarton Oaks Research Library and Collection, 1984).

Malmberg, Simon, 'Dazzling Dining: Banquets as an Expression of Imperial Legitimacy', in Kalirroe Linardou and Leslie Brubaker (Eds.), *Eat, Drink andBe Merry (Luke 12:19): Food and Wine in Byzantium. Papers of the 37th Annual Spring Symposium of Byzantine Studies, In Honour of Professor A.A.M. Bryer* (Aldershot: Ashgate, 2007), 75–91.

Malmberg, Simon, 'Visualising Hierarchy at Imperial Banquets', in Wendy Mayer and Silke Trzcionka (eds.), *Feast, Fast or Famine. Food and Drink in Byzantium* (Leiden: Brill, 2005), 11–24.

Mamboury, Ernest and Theodor Wiegand, *Die Kaiserpaläste von Konstantinopel zwischen Hippodrom und Marmara-Meer* (Berlin: De Gruyter, 1934).

Mango, Cyril, 'Ancient Spolia in the Great Palace of Constantinople', in Doula Mouriki (ed.), *Byzantine East, Latin West: Art Historical Studies in Honor of Kurt Weitzmann* (Princeton: Princeton University Press, 1995), 645–657.

Mango, Cyril, *The Brazen House: A Study on the Vestibule of the Imperial Palace of Constantinople* (Copenhagen: I kommission hos Munksgaard, 1959).

Mango, Cyril, 'Constantinopolitana', *Jahrbuch des Deutschen Archäologischen Instituts* 80 (1965): 305–336.

Mango, Cyril, 'The Palace of the Boukoleon', *Cahiers archéologiques, fin de l'Antiquité et Moyen Âge* 45 (1997): 41–50.

Mango, Cyril and Irving Lavin, 'David Talbot Rice, ed., The Great Palace of the Byzantine Emperors, Edinburgh University Press, 1958', *The Art Bulletin* 42 (1969): 67–73.

Mango, Marlia M., 'Polychrome Tiles Found at Istanbul: Typology, Chronology and Function', in Sharon E. J. Gerstel and Julie Lauffenburger (eds.), *A Lost Art Rediscovered: The Architectural Ceramics of Byzantium* (Baltimore: Walters Art Museum-Pennsylvania University Press, 2001), 13–41.

McClary, Richard P., *Rum Seljuq Architecture, 1170–1220: The Patronage of Sultans* (Edinburgh: Edinburgh University Press, 2017).

McCormick, Michael, 'Analyzing Imperial Ceremonies', *Jahrbuch der Österreichischen Byzantinistik* 35 (1985): 1–20.

Miranda, Salvador, 'Étude sur le Palais Sacré de Constantinople: Le Walker Trust et le Palais de Daphnè', *Byzantinoslavica* 44 (1983): 41–49.

Morss, Chuck, 'The Family of the Great Palace Mosaic', *Byzantine Studies Conference Archives* (1998) [https://bsana.net/conference/archives/1998/abstracts_1998.php, retrieved 3 January 2021].

Nordhagen, Per J., 'The Mosaics of the Great Palace of the Byzantine Emperors', *Byzantinische Zeitschrift* 56, 1 (1963): 53–68.

Ousterhout, Robert, 'Reconstructing Ninth-Century Constantinople', in Leslie Brubaker (ed.), *Byzantium in the Ninth Century: Dead or Alive?* (London: Routledge, 2016), 116–124.

Parker, Grant, *The Making of Roman India* (Cambridge: Cambridge University Press, 2008).

Pasinli, Alpay, 'La zona settentrionale del Gran Palazzo: Interventi di scavo. Il Giardino della vecchia prigione di Sultanahmet', in Eugenia Bolognesi (ed.), *Il Gran Palazzo degli Imperatori di Bisanzio* (Rome: Istituto Italiano di Cultura di Istanbul, 2000), 37–45.

Pasinli, Alpay, 'Pittakia ve Magnum Palatium-Büyük Saray Bölgesinde 1999 Yili Çalışmaları (Eski Sultanahmet Cezaevi Bahçesi)', *Müze Çalışmaları* 11 (2001): 41–64.

Pasinli, Alpay, 'Pittakia ve Magnum Palatium-Büyük Saray Bölgesinde 2000 Yili Çalışmaları (Eski Sultanahmet Cezaevi Bahçesi)', *Müze Çalışmaları* 12 (2002): 1–22.

Pasinli, Alpay, 'Pittakia ve Magnum Palatium-Büyük Saray Bölgesinde 2001 Yili Çalışmaları (Eski Sultanahmet Cezaevi Bahçesi)', *Müze Çalışmaları* 13 (2003): 1–16.

Pattenden, Philip, 'The Byzantine Early Warning System', *Byzantion* 53, 1 (1983): 258–299.

Perich Roca, Arnau, 'El palacio de Qasr ibn Wardan (Siria) y la evolución de la tipología palacial bizantina (siglos VI–XV)', *Revista d'arqueologia de Ponent* 23 (2013): 45–74.

Piccirillo, Michele and Eugenio Alliata, *Mount Nebo: New Archaeological Excavations, 1967–1997*, 2 vols. (Jerusalem: Stadium Biblicum Franciscanum, 1998).

Piraud-Fournet, Pauline, 'Le Palais de Trajan à Bosra: Présentation et hypothèses d'identification', *Syria* 80 (2003): 5–40.

Popović, Ivana, 'Porphyry sculptures from Sirmium', *Antiquité Tardive* 24 (2016): 373–374.

Popović, Vladislav and Edward L. Ochsenschlager, 'Der spätkaiserzeitliche Hippodrom in Sirmium', *Germania* 54, 1 (1976): 156–181.

*Reallexikon für Antike und Christentum*, supplement 11 (Stuttgart: Anton Hiersemann, 2004).

Rollinger, Christian, *Zeremoniell und Herrschaft in der Spätantike: Die Rituale des Kaiserhofs in Konstantinopel* (Stuttgart: Franz Steiner Verlag, 2024).

Schneider, Pierre, *L'Éthiopie et l'Inde: Interférences et confusions aux extrémités du monde antique* (VIIIe siècle avant J.-C.-VIe siècle de notre ère) (Rome: École Française de Rome, 2004).

Sodini, Jean-Pierre, 'Habitat de l'antiquité tardive (1)', *Topoi* 5, 1 (1995): 151–218.

Sodini, Jean-Pierre, 'Habitat de l'antiquité tardive (2)', *Topoi* 7, 2 (1997): 435–577.

Stichel, Rudolf, 'Sechs kolossale Säulen nahe der Hagia Sophia und die Curia Justinians am Augusteion in Konstantinopel', *Architectura* 30 (2000): 1–25.

Talbot Rice, David, *The Great Palace of the Byzantine Emperors: Second Report* (Edinburgh: Edinburgh University Press, 1958).

Toynbee, Jocelyn M. C. and Kenneth S. Painter, 'Silver Picture Plates of Late Antiquity: A.D. 300 to 700', *Archaeologia* 108 (1986): 15–65.

Trilling, James, 'The Soul of the Empire: Style and Meaning in the Mosaic Pavement of the Byzantine Imperial Palace in Constantinople', *Dumbarton Oaks Papers* 43 (1989): 27–72.

Tülek, Füsun, 'A Fifth Century Floor Mosaic and a Mural of Virgin of Pege in Constantinople', *Cahiers archéologiques, fin de l'Antiquité et Moyen Âge* 52 (2009): 23–30.

Turcan, Robert, *Les sarcophages romains à représentations dionysiaques: Essai de chronologie et d'histoire religieuse* (Paris: De Boccard, 1966).

Van Millingen, Alexander, *Byzantine Constantinople: The Walls of the City and Adjoining Historical Sites* (London: J. Murray, 1899).

Vendries, Christophe, 'L'auceps, les gluaux et l'appeau: La ruse du chasseur d'oiseaux', in Jean Trinquier and Christophe Vendries (eds.), *Chasses antiques* (Rennes: Presses Universitaires de Rennes, 2009), 119–140.

Walker, Alicia, *The Emperor and the World: Exotic Elements and the Imaging of Middle Byzantine Imperial Power, Ninth to Thirteenth Centuries C.E.* (Cambridge: Cambridge University Press, 2012).

Weitzmann, Kurt and George Galavaris, *The Monastery of Saint Catherine at Mount Sinai: The Illuminated Greek Manuscripts*, vol. 1 (Princeton: Princeton University Press, 1990).

Westbrook, Nigel, 'Exchange of Palatine Architectural Motifs between Byzantium, Persia and the Caliphate', in Danijel Dzino and Ken Parry (eds.), *Byzantium, its Neighbours and its Cultures* (Leiden: Brill, 2017), 129–153.

Westbrook, Nigel, *The Great Palace of Constantinople: An Architectural Interpretation* (Turnhout: Brepols, 2019).

Whitby, Mary, 'The Great Palace Dig: The Scottish Perspective', in Robin Cormack and Elizabeth Jeffreys (eds.), *Through the Looking Glass: Byzantium Through British Eyes* (London: Routledge, 2000), 45–66.

Wright, David H., 'The Shape of the Seventh Century in Byzantine Art', in *First Annual Byzantine Studies Conference Abstracts of Papers* (Cleveland: 1975), 9–28.

# Cambridge Elements

## The History of Constantinople

### Peter Frankopan
*University of Oxford*

Peter Frankopan is Professor of Global History at Oxford University, where he is also Director of the Centre for Byzantine Research and Senior Research Fellow at Worcester College. He specialises in the history of the Eastern Mediterranean from antiquity to the modern day, and is the author of the best-sellers *The Silk Roads: A New History of the World* (2015) and *The New Silk Roads:* The Future and Present of the World (2018).

### About the Series

Telling the history of Constantinople through its monuments and people, leading scholars present a rich and unbiased account of this ever-evolving metropolis. From its foundation to the domination of the Ottoman Empire to contemporary Istanbul, numerous aspects of Constantinople's narrative are explored in this unrivalled series.

# Cambridge Elements

## The History of Constantinople

### Elements in the Series

*The Statues of Constantinople*
Albrecht Berger

*The Hippodrome of Constantinople*
Engin Akyürek

*The Church of St. Polyeuktos at Constantinople*
Fabian Stroth

*The Chora Monastery of Constantinople*
Emmanuel S. Moutafov

*The Great Palace*
Alfredo Calahorra Bartolomé

A full series listing is available at www.cambridge.org/EHCO

For EU product safety concerns, contact us at Calle de José Abascal, 56–1°, 28003 Madrid, Spain or eugpsr@cambridge.org.

www.ingramcontent.com/pod-product-compliance
Lightning Source LLC
LaVergne TN
LVHW021948060526
838200LV00043B/1958